PRAISES FOR

THE CAREGIVER'S JOURNEY

"In my role as a physician caring for a largely elderly population, I have found that there are few challenges that can confront a family [that are] as confusing and intimidating as dealing with the progressive physical and mental decline of a loved one. What is to be expected? What resources are available? Where can reliable information be obtained? In his new book, *The Caregiver's Journey: Compassionate and Informed Care for a Loved One*, Todd Cope has provided an information-packed, concise, and readable reference for the caregiver facing this challenge. I highly recommend this book to any who are involved in the care of the frail elderly.

—Bruce Chamberlain, MD, FACP, FAAHPM

"Taking care of a loved one can be overwhelming, confusing, and cause feelings of despair and loneliness. As a hospice nurse with twenty years of experience, it has been a challenge to find a resource that offers a practical approach to caregiving. *The Caregiver's Journey: Compassionate and Informed Care for a Loved One* provides education and support to those who are facing one of the most difficult times in their lives. Todd Cope reminds caregivers to continue living and that humor is 'good medicine.' I highly recommend this book to anyone caring for a loved one. I'm convinced you will find it informative and refreshing."

—Carma Karsten RN, CHPN

the

CAREGIVER'S

Journey

Compassionate and Informed
Care for a Loved One

the CAREGIVER'S *Journey*

Compassionate and Informed Care for a Loved One

Todd F. Cope, RN

Plain Sight Publishing
An Imprint of Cedar Fort, Inc.
Springville, Utah

ISBN 13: 978-1-4621-1677-5

Published by Plain Sight Publishing, an imprint of Cedar Fort, Inc.
2373 W. 700 S., Springville, UT 84663
Distributed by Cedar Fort, Inc., www.cedarfort.com

Library of Congress Cataloging-in-Publication Data
Cope, Todd F., author.
The caregiver's journey / Todd F. Cope, RN.
    pages cm
Includes bibliographical references.
ISBN 978-1-4621-1677-5
1. Aging parents--Care. I. Title.

HQ1063.6.C685 2015
306.874084'6--dc23

2015008245

Cover design by Angela Decker
Cover design © 2015 by Lyle Mortimer
Edited and typeset by Eileen Leavitt

Printed in the United States of America

10 9 8 7 6 5 4 3 2 1

Printed on acid-free paper

To Bill Eckhardt, whose encouragement, devotion,
and humility will always be remembered.

CONTENTS

FOREWORD

With the increasing number of people finding themselves as informal caregivers of aging family members, there is a growing demand for caregiver resources. Many families in the United States have an older loved one requiring care, and the number of family caregivers is only expected to increase. Family caregivers are often desperate for accurate and useful information in a convenient format. While there are many books available to assist caregivers in their responsibilities, and each likely has strengths, most sources seem packed with information that is difficult to digest, especially within the limited time that caregivers have to look for information.

The Caregiver's Journey: Compassionate and Informed Care for a Loved One is a perfect resource for caregivers because it presents helpful information in an engaging way that is easy to follow. Caregiving principles are interwoven with stories to give caregivers real-life examples of how to address difficult situations.

Todd Cope, a registered nurse for more than two decades and a family caregiver for both of his parents, has written some of the things he has learned about caregiving so that you, as a caregiver, might have some direction in this challenging endeavor. Todd personally understands what you as a caregiver may be experiencing. He has lived through those long and sleepless nights and knows how it feels to be called away from work to deal with a crisis. His unique perspective as both a personal and professional caregiver allows him to provide informed and helpful advice and lends strong credibility to this book.

Whether you are just beginning the caregiving journey or are somewhere along the way, *The Caregiver's Journey* provides a sensitive and informed perspective of caregiving experiences. Powerful concepts and real-life examples are woven into a detailed portrait of the caregiving journey. I have taught about caregiving to university students for several years. I loved reading this book because Todd provides a springboard for new caregivers to know the main issues along with resources to meet the challenges that many caregivers face. Some of the gems in this book include simple solutions to behavior problems, suggestions for difficult decisions (including those made at the end of life), appropriate expectations of self and other caregivers (informal and formal caregivers), and good advice in difficult situations. Todd sensitively addresses the many emotions of caregiving. He frankly addresses anticipated difficulties and helps the reader to consider the many blessings of providing care to a loved one. I most highly recommend this book to caregivers who are starting the journey or are seeking help in navigating challenges associated with caring for a loved one.

As the number of people living into their eighth and ninth decades increases, so will the need for qualified caregivers grow. This book is an ideal source for information that will help prepare anyone who is or may be called upon to provide care to a loved one. It offers a solid foundation for family caregivers, regardless of where they are along the path of caregiving.

Dr. Jeremy B. Yorgason
Associate Professor
School of Family Life
Brigham Young University

PREFACE

"Accept the challenges so that you
may feel the exhilaration of victory."[1]
—General George S. Patton

O ne of the most frequent comments I hear when visiting with new caregivers of the elderly is, "There is nowhere to get information about how to do this." While this statement may not be completely accurate, the sentiment is certainly appreciated. Many resources for those involved in caring for the elderly seem to focus on providing care for those in the advanced stages of dementia, particularly Alzheimer's disease, while others provide large quantities of information that may seem overwhelming to a new caregiver. These resources can provide invaluable insight for seasoned caregivers who desire more detailed information, but clearly, new caregivers do not fall into this category. Many people start being a caregiver by simply assisting a relative or friend who is dealing with the complexities of advancing age. Whether they assist with simple financial matters or provide full-scale personal care, they usually become caregivers without even realizing it. It is in these early stages of realization that most unsuspecting caregivers find themselves wanting *simple* resources to prepare them for the road ahead.

It is with you and other new caregivers that I wish to share my insights. My hope is to assist in bridging the gap between the instinctual ability for basic care that most of us possess and the advanced care for which there are already multiple resources available. Most of what I share is anecdotal rather than scientific, and it comes from many years of experience as a registered nurse and the personal experience of caring for elderly loved ones rather than from years of data collection and analysis. I offer the qualitative human side of caring and leave to others the quantitative aspect of providing care. You will notice a list of notes and references in chapter three for the section on general age-related problems. These references simply confirm my observations over many years as a nurse. In addition, those notes include Internet resources where you can find additional information regarding the more prevalent forms of dementia.

There is no way to provide all the answers, nor is there time to seek them, but my desire is to provide enough insight within the relatively few pages that follow to help you come up with the answers you need. It is not my expectation that you will agree with every suggestion I offer, but it is my hope that every suggestion will assist you in finding the right way to deal with your specific circumstance. The information I provide and experiences I share should lay a solid foundation upon which you can build. Though the specific experiences are unique to those involved, and the choices they made may differ from those you would make, the general principles associated with each experience can be applied (or at least considered) if the time comes that you find yourself in a similar situation.

If you are someone who has found yourself involved, in any way, in the care of an elderly person, like it or not, you are a caregiver. As a caregiver, if you feel confused, overwhelmed, or both, this book is intended for you. In personal, simple, and sometimes humorous terms, I offer the content that follows as a means of helping you gain confidence in your abilities, comfort in times of need, and hope in the future.

NOTES

1.	George S. Patton, quoted in William F. Moloney and Lincoln Grindle, *Textbook of Phacoemulsification* (Fallbrook, CA: Lasenda Publishing, 1988), 79.

INTRODUCTION

When my children were young, I remember becoming frustrated when we would be traveling as a family and at some point not far into our journey, one of the children would ask, "Are we there yet?" I wanted to say, "Obviously, we're not, or we would have stopped." But, trying to be a patient parent, I would respond with something like, "No, we're not there, we're here." I thought I was being funny. The child, however, just stared at me blankly and soon repeated the question. At this point, I usually resorted to sarcasm. "Yep, we're finally here at mile marker sixty-three. Now let's pull over and have some fun!" My clever mockery went unappreciated, and invariably the question was asked again. Of course, this process continued until I was at my wit's end, and the child still wondered if we were there yet.

"Are we there yet?" seems to be a universally annoying question for parents, yet how many have actually considered why their child asks? I know I hadn't until I began working with the elderly. I often found myself in the middle of a difficult day, looking forward to—I wasn't sure what—and wanting to ask my colleagues that very question: "Are we there yet?" The reason I wanted to ask was the same reason my child asked; though aware of what journey we were on, neither of us knew just what to expect en route, nor did we know exactly what it would be like when we reached the end.

Had I been a wise parent, our family trips to new places could have been free of the dreaded question. All I needed to do was prepare my children before the journey began and keep them informed along the way. In addition to telling them where we were going, I could have told them of landmarks and points of interest we could expect to see as we traveled, as well as possible detours or things that might prolong the journey. Then if the question, "Are we there yet?" was raised, it would have been a simple matter of reminding them of what they might still expect to see before we arrived. So it is with the journey we call caregiving. As you are transformed into a caregiver for an elderly loved one, you embark on a journey through unfamiliar territory to an unfamiliar destination. You are bound to ask, "Are we there yet?" with each new unsuspected twist or challenge unless you're prepared for the journey.

The purpose of this book is to prepare you, as a potentially apprehensive caregiver, for the challenges ahead as you begin or continue this rewarding journey. I hope to provide some tools that will minimize the number of times you feel like asking the question, "Are we there yet?" As your journey proceeds, you will probably still find yourself occasionally muttering the words under your breath before you will realize that you actually have an idea of what the answer might be. In time, many of the answers will be there before the question is asked.

The stories and experiences I share are real. They happened to people just like you or those for whom you care. In order to protect privacy, I have taken the liberty of changing names and adapting other information that could be used to identify those involved. It may seem to some that the stories I have chosen to include lean toward the more negative aspects of caregiving. While this is not the specific intent, I do understand how that conclusion could be drawn. Challenges are part of caregiving, and any attempt to ignore that fact or minimize it would defeat the purpose of this book. But while there may be some negative aspects in the stories, there are also positive aspects in each one. My encouragement would be to recognize and learn from both aspects as you read and experience similar situations on your journey.

Throughout the book, I use the term *loved one* when referring to those who are receiving care from a caregiver. This term is not intended to imply that all caregivers should be or are immediate or extended family members to the one receiving care. Rather, *loved one* is used as a general term that I believe is appropriate in all situations because the care you provide should be based, at least in part, on love. This, therefore, makes the one you are caring for a loved one, whether or not you are related.

Part 1

"Don't cry because it's over.
Smile because it happened."
—Anonymous proverb

FREQUENT
DELAYS

There seem to always be some last-minute delays that prevent you from setting out on any long journey; then, once you are on your way, further delays often impede your progress. Stopping at the store for ice or the gas station to put air in the tires before leaving town often means you leave later than you had planned. As you start off once again, you may realize that you failed to cancel an appointment and need to pull over to make a phone call. Perhaps you find yourself more tired than you realized and need to stop for a brief nap or to change drivers. Maybe you thought you knew where you were going but soon discover things don't look familiar or the route isn't as simple as you thought it was, so you have to stop and review the map one more time.

Most of us have experienced these setbacks during the early stages of a big trip. Similarly, you can expect delays as you begin your journey as a caregiver. While it would be nice for everything to go as planned, there will always be challenges. The more time and energy you use to focus on these early challenges, the longer it takes for you to establish a care routine. The chapters in this section address the common challenges that most caregivers face that can potentially distract from the care of a loved one.

Chapter one explores ways to manage the feelings of guilt often experienced by caregivers. Chapter two addresses ways to avoid carrying too much of the caregiving load alone. Chapter three provides a brief explanation of the challenges that result from the aging process and the basic care techniques that will help you cope with them.

Chapter 1

MOVING ON

MANAGING FEELINGS
OF GUILT

Delia was a wonderful neighbor. From the time she moved onto Carter Street, hers was the house all the neighborhood children loved to frequent. Whether she was telling elaborately detailed Christmas stories or dressing up as the spookiest witch on Halloween, Delia was part of each child's life. Every adult in the neighborhood knew that Delia's ear was always available for listening and her shoulder was always there to cry on. No one ever visited her without being treated to some of her famous cooking. Delia's hospitality seemed never ending. That's why everyone was so willing to help her when she needed it. But as time passed and Delia grew older, she began to call on her neighbors for more and more things—to the point that she expected them to meet all of her needs.

In desperation, a concerned neighbor finally contacted Delia's out-of-town sister and closest family member, Anne. She explained to Anne that the neighbors were happy to help Delia when they could but that she had become demanding, even calling people in the middle of the night for things that could have waited. Delia's requests had moved beyond things like picking up a few groceries to driving her to visit a friend three hours away.

Anne was grateful for the call and was understanding. She arranged for Delia to be seen by her doctor, who diagnosed Delia with dementia. Anne was able to hire a part-time caregiver to spend time with Delia and help her with household tasks and to run errands and pay bills. In addition, Anne was able to recruit the help of extended family members who lived nearby and who were excited about getting reacquainted with Aunt Delia. With this additional help and the willingness of the neighbors to still assist when they could, Delia had someone checking with her at least daily. These arrangements worked wonderfully for a time, but as Delia's dementia increased, so did her needs. Her employed caregiver began to notice that checks were being written to unfamiliar people, and concerns for Delia's safety began to surface.

One morning, the caregiver arrived to find Delia's house filled with smoke. She rushed to the kitchen, where she discovered a burning dish towel in the oven. Delia was still asleep in her bed and was fine, but things could have turned out much differently. When Anne was informed of the situation, she conferred with Delia's doctor, who agreed that it was time for Delia to have someone with her all the time.

After a great deal of contemplation and discussion with extended family, Anne determined that the best way to meet Delia's needs was to move her to an assisted living facility. Anne found a place near enough to Delia's home that her neighbors could visit occasionally, and it was even close enough for Anne to visit once a week. Delia was not happy about the move and complained that she was just fine in her home. Each time Anne visited, Delia let her know how unhappy she was. She didn't understand why Anne wouldn't let her move back home under the previous arrangements. Anne tried to explain that it was just too much for family and friends to meet Delia's needs and keep her safe. Still, Delia complained.

Anne found herself in tears after each visit with her sister. She felt burdened with guilt because she wasn't doing more. She began exploring ways to make additional visits with Delia and even contemplated having Delia move in with her. Upon recognizing his mother's feelings of guilt, one of Anne's sons had a frank but caring discussion with her. He pointed out that there was no reason that Anne should feel guilty, because not only was she doing everything she could for her sister, she was also doing what was best for her. He helped his mother recognize that because of her own advanced age, she, like Delia, was dependent upon others for many of her needs, and any additional responsibilities Anne accepted automatically became the responsibility of those she depended on. Anne eventually accepted that her guilt was unnecessary and would only lead to unfair expectations of others. Delia never did stop complaining, but Anne recognized that she was doing what was best for her sister, in spite of the grumbling.

Difficult Decisions

There are many challenges that accompany caring for an aging adult. As you transition into the role of caregiver, you will quickly discover that making decisions is one of the greatest challenges you will face. Unless you are someone who is indecisive about everything, decision making itself is not difficult. The difficulty arises when you realize the impact your decisions may have on someone else's sense of independence. This realization, coupled with the anger sometimes expressed by your loved one when they perceive loss, can lead to feelings of guilt on your part. It is natural to question a decision you have made when someone expresses anger toward you because of it. This can lead to second-guessing yourself and allowing feelings of guilt to consume you.

If your loved one reaches the point that his or her health or safety, in any form, depends on help from someone else, you must act in whatever way is necessary to keep him or her healthy and safe. Some people may be reluctant to take such steps for fear of ignoring the wishes of their loved one, thereby taking advantage of someone's vulnerability or forcing an opinion on another adult. While these concerns on the part of a caregiver may be understandable, they do not take into account the alternative. To do nothing in circumstances where your loved one could harm him- or herself or someone else would be negligent. Some aging adults are able to admit to themselves and their family that they could benefit from additional help in meeting some of their needs and they are willing to give up some independence to receive it. Others, however, find it more difficult. These needs are usually first identified by a caregiver, who in turn starts the discussion regarding care assistance. It is not hard to understand why seniors are slow to recognize or admit to the need for help from someone else, especially if the needed help is of a very personal nature or requires giving up some independence. Your loved one should be involved in making these care decisions to the extent possible. His or her input should always be sought and honored as long as health and safety will not be jeopardized. This can be difficult, especially if you have differing opinions about how the identified care needs can best be met, but consensus should be the goal. Remember that your way may not always be the best way and is probably not the only way. Be willing to compromise as long as doing so will not put your loved one in harm's way.

It has been my experience that those accepting assistance when they first need it require less help over time than those who wait until they have no choice before receiving help. Life expectancy may not increase, but quality of life certainly will. Explaining this concept to a resistant loved one may help him or her come to terms with a care choice that may not be preferred but is best.

If your loved one suffers from dementia, the same basic concepts of arranging for appropriate care apply. You should involve him or her in the decision-making process to the extent that he or she is cognitively capable. Even if your loved one is not able to make a safe decision, he or she should be included in the discussions and offered an explanation for each decision.

When you arrange for or provide help for a resistant loved one in need, be prepared for some unexpected responses from both you and that person. You may feel that you are forcing your opinion on your loved one and may wonder if you have done the right thing. Questioning and second-guessing are common responses in this circumstance but are not sufficient reasons to leave your loved one in need. Avoiding the issue will not make it disappear and could lead to harm. If you find yourself facing this challenge, consider the following as a measure for your justification in having made a necessary and perhaps, the only reasonable decision: Did you consider your loved one's input and implement as much of his or her desire as possible? Was the final decision necessary to assure your loved one's health and safety? If you answer yes to both of these questions, you have done the right thing.

In spite of your sound reason and justification, decisions made on behalf of these resistant loved ones in need may still be negatively interpreted by them. Even if they recognize the benefits, dependent elderly adults sometimes, understandably, develop feelings of inadequacy and the sense that they are losing their independence when they rely on someone else for any of their needs. A frequent reaction to this loss of independence, whether perceived or real, can be anger toward you, the caregiver. Do not make the mistake of believing you are the cause of their dependence when you simply identified a care need. If you find yourself caring for an angry loved one, just remember, their anger does not change their need for assistance, though it can create feelings of guilt on your part.

Guilt is a natural emotion and can be a healthy motivator if kept in perspective. But I have witnessed caregivers who cultivate and dwell on these feelings of guilt to the point that the feelings grow to an unhealthy level. When guilt takes control of your emotions, you may find it difficult to make the necessary hard decisions to meet your loved one's needs and to assure his or her health and safety. Rather than allowing guilt to prevent you from arranging for or providing needed care for your loved one, use it to motivate you to appropriate action.

If you found yourself in the situation your loved one is now facing, you too would likely be frustrated and perhaps even angry. As difficult as it may be, especially in the heat of the moment, try to reflect on how your loved one feels. Keep things in perspective, and try to remember what motivates you to be a caregiver. Always do your best to consider and understand your loved one's circumstances and feelings.

As a caregiver, you will make mistakes. It is not uncommon to carefully

Did you consider your loved one's input and implement as much of his or her desire as possible? Was the final decision necessary to assure your loved one's health and safety? If you answer yes to both of these questions, you have done the right thing.

and thoughtfully make care decisions that later prove to be less helpful to your loved one than you had hoped. These situations can lead to guilt, but they can also generate opportunities for reflection that will, in turn, lead to corrective action. You may not be able to reverse a past mistake, but you can avoid making similar ones in the future. While perfection in caregiving may not be possible, it should still be the goal. Every caregiver should welcome any opportunity to improve, and these opportunities often come in the form of mistakes. Once you accept the fact that you will make mistakes, you can turn them into assets rather than liabilities by following these simple steps: recognize that you made a mistake, make any necessary immediate corrections or adjustments to protect your loved one, and avoid any future repeats.

I need to mention another emotion that caregivers sometimes experience when making difficult decisions for a dependent loved one. Though it may seem out of place, grief can accompany guilt. When your loved one accepts help, thus giving up independence, he or she experiences loss. You might experience a similar loss when you make arrangements for or provide the help they need. This process represents a change in who your loved one is to you; your relationship changes. In a very real sense, you could be grieving the loss of your loved one. While he or she is not gone, the changes you see in your loved one's life can result in this unexpected form of grief. Just like guilt, grief is a natural emotion that has a useful place in your life. It can be a healthy emotional outlet when kept in perspective. As you know, when any emotion begins to control your life, it is probably out of perspective. The best advice I can offer if you find yourself facing this form of grief is: don't let *what* your loved one has become make you forget *who* he or she is. Try to identify the changes in your loved one and recognize and accept any accompanying grief for what it is. Once they are accepted, these emotions can be harnessed and used as a means of motivation for providing appropriate care for your loved one rather than becoming a distraction.

Genuine Concern: The Basis for All Decisions

If you find yourself feeling guilty about taking the steps necessary to make life better for your loved one, remember that guilt implies wrong-doing. Making the tough decisions that ensure the best care is never the wrong choice. Still, it is difficult when you know you have made the best decision you could, yet find others questioning your reasons or motivation.

If you are the designated decision maker regarding a loved one's care, you can avoid excessive feelings of guilt by remembering one thing. If you make every decision based on genuine concern, with no selfish or ulterior motive, you have made the right decision. This does not mean that you will never discover, in hindsight, that you may have made a different decision if you had had the additional information or knowledge that you now possess, but even then, if it was made within the parameters of genuine concern, it was correct at the time. If others trust you to make decisions and you do your best to make the right ones, you can be confident in your decision making process. With genuine concern as the basis for all of your decisions, any occasional mistake will be appropriately dealt with, and your loved one's needs will continue to be met with minimal interruption.

In most situations, the primary caregiver is also the decision maker, but there are times when someone else or even several people are involved. Experience has proven that it is more difficult for several people to come together and make appropriate care decisions than when there is one person who has the final say. It is usually best for your loved one when several people are involved in the discussion, but then the final decision is left to one trusted caregiver. If your circumstance is such that more than one decision maker is involved, it is crucial that all of you are united in all decisions. Any dissension could result in substandard care for your loved one and frustration for you.

Chapter 2

DRIVER FATIGUE
SHARING THE HEAVY LOAD

Karl had been an active man all his life. As a high school coach, he knew about hard work and determination, but when he was diagnosed with a degenerative nerve disorder, things changed. Suddenly, his drive and determination weren't sufficient to overcome the challenges he now faced.

It was difficult for Linda to watch her husband slowly lose his independence, but she was confident that with her help, Karl could meet his new challenge.

The couple discussed the future and agreed that together, they could handle anything that came their way. They knew their finances were limited, but they were determined to make it without imposing on anyone else.

For several years, they got along quite well. Though there were difficult times, neither of them ever complained. Even their children were unaware of some of the more difficult challenges the couple faced and overcame together. But as Karl's condition progressed and his strength decreased, Linda found that the physical demands on her were increasing. Still, they managed.

One day, Karl fell out of his wheelchair. He had become so weak that he was unable to assist Linda as she attempted to get him off the floor. They struggled for several hours with no success. Finally, one of their children stopped by and was able to provide the needed assistance. He was concerned with what he found and asked why they had not called for his help. Linda assured her son that there had been no need to bother him or anyone else and that this had been an isolated incident. She insisted that they would be fine.

Each day grew more difficult for Karl and Linda, but because of the experience with the wheelchair, the family began paying closer attention. They realized that their parents needed help and arranged for someone in the family to stop in each day. Though Karl and Linda still refused any assistance, at least their children were able to more closely monitor the situation.

It seemed that no amount of arguing could convince Karl or Linda that they needed additional help. Then one day, Linda became ill. That evening, when one of the children found both parents still in bed, she recognized that the situation had reached a crisis stage. The family kindly but firmly insisted that their parents accept outside help. Though their circumstances limited how much additional help they could offer, the family was able to contact Karl's doctor and make arrangements for home health. As a family, they continued to stop in each day and make sure everyone was okay.

In time, Linda came to appreciate the extra help with Karl as her own health improved. Karl, too, admitted that he felt safer when he wasn't relying wholly on Linda.

Caregiver Burnout

Caregiving is hard work. It is mentally, physically, and emotionally taxing. Few people are strong enough to carry this load alone. As a caregiver, you must be prepared for when it is time to seek additional help with your loved one. People often ask how to recognize that time. Typically, if you find yourself asking whether it is time for more help, then it's time.

While you will likely feel a sense of relief when you know there is someone to assist you as a caregiver, you may sense a loss of independence (just like your loved one) as you recognize that you are now depending on someone else to help with their care. Then perhaps you wonder if you have given up at a time of weakness or if you are simply being selfish. You may even say to yourself, "I probably acted prematurely," or, "I could have hung on a little longer." But try to remember that these feelings are usually the result of your own sense of obligation or your loved one's expressions of anger or frustration, not your having done something wrong.

At this point, step back and remember why you sought additional help. Hopefully

Typically, if you find yourself asking whether it is time for more help, then it's time.

it was because you recognized that you needed it. Don't ever think that it is selfish to consider your own health while caring for a loved one. Ruining your own health because you feel an obligation to "do it on your own" or because you feel guilty about involving others simply makes you an additional burden to someone else when you work so hard that your own health fails. At that point, you too begin requiring assistance with your needs.

Times Have Changed

Many of us were raised in a culture where we were taught that we must "care for our own." We may even have memories of a grandparent or an extended family member who lived with us or another relative in his or her declining years. These societal practices are still part of many cultures in the world, and there is nothing wrong with them. In fact, they should be celebrated. But not everyone is in a situation to care for loved ones in this way.

There was a time in Western culture when the father supported the family by working on the farm or in town while the mother stayed home with the children. This common family structure was an ideal situation for a grandparent to move in with the family when he or she needed help. But that time existed when circumstances seldom required the mother to work outside of the home. It was before carpools were necessary to take children to the school a mile from home and across two major highways. It preceded teenagers having jobs at the mall in the next town and needing a ride to and from work every afternoon. In short, times have changed, and for most of us, so have the circumstances.

While there are still some people who are able to care for elderly loved ones at home, this is becoming a rarity. With the availability of many quality options for care, there is no need for a family to be negatively disrupted because of a sense of duty or a perceived obligation to care for an elderly loved one at home. When such arrangements are made simply to avoid feelings of guilt, they often result in substandard care, caregiver burnout, and family resentment. The end result is that everyone loses.

Financial Considerations

As much as we may wish it were otherwise, finances generally have to be considered when arranging care for your loved one. While some families have the financial means to provide whatever care is needed, no matter what the cost, most have to watch their pennies. The cost of care for your loved one will depend on the type of care he or she needs and the length of time the care will be needed. No two situations are exactly alike, so it pays to be prepared for whatever the future may hold for your love one's circumstances. All available options should be explored.

Many seniors have long-term care insurance policies that are designed to help finance care in the retirement years. If your loved one has such a policy, you will need to know the terms of the policy and the types of care it will pay for. Most of these policies have strict rules and limits, so a clear understanding and careful planning will be necessary to take full advantage of the benefits.

Some types of life insurance, such as Whole Life or Universal Life, offer a cash benefit or the option to take out a loan against the policy. If your loved one has such a policy and has been paying into it for many years, there may be a sufficient amount of money available to assist in meeting some of his or her care needs, even if only for a limited time.

Veteran's benefits may be available to help pay for some of your loved one's care. Available benefits can extend beyond the veteran to a surviving spouse. If your loved one is a veteran or the surviving spouse of a veteran of any branch of the United States military, he or she may qualify for financial benefits.

Your loved one's current assets may need to be used to help finance his or her care. Depending on their specific care needs, this could range from selling an unused vehicle to renting or selling his or her home.

In some cases, the financial aspects of providing care are straightforward, but they can be quite complicated. Many seniors employ a qualified financial planner who is able to help explore financial needs, or there may be a family member who is skilled in finances and is willing to take care of the details. If neither of these options exists in your situation, then I recommend contacting a certified financial planner for seniors. The planner will be able to help you navigate all the options and can even work with banks, insurance companies, the Veterans Administration or realtors as necessary. As in all things that involve money, be sure you are comfortable with the reputation of anyone who assists in your loved one's financial matters.

A Word of Caution

Even the most prepared caregivers experience times when they simply feel overwhelmed. When you're tired and feel like you can't keep up, it's easy to become irritated by the demands of your loved one's care. It is natural to occasionally feel this way and is often just a warning that you need to take a break. When these warning feelings are appropriately acknowledged and dealt with, they can actually lead to a healthy release of tension. Unfortunately, caregivers can get caught up in the pressure of these situations and instead of recognizing the warnings, allow frustrations to grow into anger. This can lead caregivers to directing their frustrations toward their loved one.

Care of a loved one should never be approached in anger. Don't yell or curse at your loved one. Avoid withholding privileges or threatening. Never hit your loved one with anything. Belittling, or speaking ill of him or her is wrong. All of these responses equate to abuse and are never appropriate.

If you find yourself using or being tempted to use any of these inappropriate reactions to your loved one, get away from the situation until you have your emotions in control. If you suspect that someone else is abusing your loved one, intervene immediately and ensure that your loved one receives needed help.

Chapter 3

KNOW WHERE YOU'RE GOING

UNDERSTANDING THE BASICS OF CARING FOR THE ELDERLY

Nola was getting along very well. She was pleased that, even though she was eighty-six, she could still do so many things for herself. Though her family had arranged to bring in meals, Nola was still able to meet most of her own personal needs. Her daughter Cheryl came nearly every day.

One day, Cheryl came for her daily visit, but Nola wasn't sitting at the kitchen table like she usually was. Cheryl called for her mother, but there was no answer. She looked in the bathroom and the bedroom but could not find Nola. Cheryl was becoming worried, but she thought she'd make one more sweep through the apartment before she panicked. When she looked in the bedroom, she noticed that the bed was not made. She walked around the bed and found Nola lying there on the floor. Nola was awake, but there was a blank stare on her face. Cheryl attempted to help her mother up, but Nola was unable to assist. Sensing the urgency of the situation, Cheryl called 911.

At the hospital, a CT scan revealed that Nola had suffered a stroke in the area of the brain stem, leaving her paralyzed from the neck down, unable to speak and unable to swallow. Remarkably, Nola seemed able to comprehend what was going on. Though her face was always expressionless, Nola was able to communicate with Cheryl by blinking her eyes.

Cheryl insisted that any discussion about Nola and her treatment be held in Nola's presence. The doctors explained the different measures that could be taken to keep Nola alive, but Nola made it clear that she wanted to go home and that nothing was to be done to prolong her life.

Though it was hard to think of letting her mother go that way, Cheryl wanted to respect her wishes. She agreed to support Nola's decision and arranged for Nola to be transported home the next day.

With no time to think about being frightened, Cheryl spent the entire evening researching all she could about strokes and caring for those who had suffered one. She telephoned a friend who had cared for her father after he had suffered a stroke and got her advice. She arranged for a neighbor who worked in a nursing home to meet her at Nola's house when Nola returned so she could go over the basics of caring for someone in Nola's condition. She fell asleep reading a book about caring for someone at the end of life.

When Nola arrived home, Cheryl had everything ready. Though she was certainly not an expert, Cheryl was as prepared as she could be. With confidence, Cheryl spent the next two and a half weeks at her mother's bedside. She sang Nola's favorite songs, read from her favorite books, and sometimes just reminisced. Occasionally they'd listen to a television program together or visit with a neighbor or friend who had dropped in.

One quiet evening, after listening to a recording of Nola's favorite music, Cheryl noticed something different in her mother's eyes. She knew it was time, and as she wiped tears from her own eyes, she was sure she saw Nola smile ever so slightly. Cheryl kissed her mother's forehead and stroked her cheek as Nola closed her eyes for the last time.

Learn All You Can

Regardless of your level of involvement as a caregiver, a frequent source of anxiety is a lack of knowledge relating to care of the elderly. If you take the time to learn a little about how to provide personal care to others and then actively participate in care, you will avoid many of the pitfalls experienced by those who just dive in with little preparation. And don't underestimate the advantage you have of knowing and understanding your loved one—a luxury that professional caregivers usually don't have and a benefit that makes up for a lot of inexperience.

With today's technological advances, information about caregiving is becoming more readily available. But be careful in choosing the source of your information. Not everything you read is true or accurate. Often, information will be offered from companies or individuals whose primary goal is to sell you something. Promises of miraculously improved health or completely restored memory should cause you to question. Generally speaking, if a product or information is only available through a "special one-time offer" or an "exclusive" ad, it's not something you should invest time and money into. In addition, not everything works for everyone in every situation. Even information obtained from friends and others who have been in a situation similar to yours needs to be carefully reviewed and adapted as necessary for your situation. The key is to obtain as much information as you can from reliable sources. You may find that you have a natural filter that helps you sort through the information and determine which applies to you and your loved one.

The best knowledge is built on a solid foundation of the basics.

General Age-Related Problems

While overall health status among the elderly varies widely, even the healthiest older adults cannot escape the natural effects of age. Whether your loved one is dealing with multiple health issues or simply age-related changes, he or she will still require your assistance for at least some things. Therefore, an awareness of the basic changes you can expect to see in your loved one will help you meet his or her needs with more patience, understanding, compassion, and confidence. The following information is only a brief overview and is in no way inclusive of all the age-related changes that you may see in your loved one. Former occupation, heredity, and lifestyle all help determine the changes that occur in our body as we age. Rather than attempt to list the problems that are not considered a normal part of aging, I will suggest that anything you notice in your loved one that goes beyond the information that follows, or that causes you concern in any way, should be addressed with the appropriate healthcare professional.

Memory

It is commonly accepted by many that memory loss is an unavoidable part of aging, but research is showing that this may not be the case. Most of us will experience a slowing of our memory as we grow older, but memory loss is not a foregone conclusion.[1]

Vision

At about the age of forty, it is common for eyesight to weaken. This is the point that people begin having difficulty seeing close objects or small print.[2] Reading glasses are usually a simple solution, though longer arms would also solve this problem. The development of cataracts often occurs after the age of fifty-five. This clouding of the lens can remain small enough not to impair vision or may become large and dense and require surgery. Cataract surgery is a safe and common surgery.[3]

Hearing

Some hearing loss is experienced with increased age. Generally, this is gradual and relates to specific tones or pitches of sound. More significant hearing loss is typically related to factors such as childhood diseases, occupational environment, and heredity.[4]

Many forms of hearing loss can be treated with hearing aids. Hearing loss that interferes with normal life should be discussed with the appropriate healthcare provider.

Dental

Age itself seems to have little impact on our teeth, but other factors result in common dental concerns as we grow older. Gums may recede and teeth may become discolored or weakened as the result of things such as lifelong dietary habits or smoking.[5] Oral health may also be negatively impacted by other health problems or associated treatments that are not directly related to advanced age.[6] Proper oral care, including regular dental exams and cleanings, is the best preventative action for people of any age.

Digestion

Problems with the digestion of food can develop as we grow older, though this is more likely the result of lifestyle changes than of aging.[7] Decreased physical activity or alteration of diet can affect the gastrointestinal tract. In addition, there is a natural decrease in the number of taste buds as we age. This affects the way food tastes and often leads to a change in eating habits.[8]

Many people experience acid reflux, or heartburn, more frequently as they age. This is due to a weakening of the muscle at the bottom of the esophagus that allows stomach acids to come into contact with the sensitive esophageal lining.[9] This condition can often be resolved by avoiding spicy foods, not eating late at night, or by sleeping with the head of the bed slightly elevated. Medications may also help when more conservative measures fail to solve the problem.[10]

Elimination

One particularly unpleasant part of growing older is a concern about bladder control. While this can be an issue for both men and women, it is women who most often complain that they are unable to control their bladder, a condition known as incontinence. This is usually caused by weakened bladder muscles and can result in problems that range from minor dribbling to severe loss of bladder control. In many cases, this type of incontinence can be treated and cured.[11]

The most common complaint from men relates to difficulty in starting and stopping a urine stream, which frequently results from an enlarged prostate gland. This enlargement is usually harmless, and symptoms can begin as early as the mid-forties. Medications can be prescribed that will help control the problem. In more severe cases, surgery may be necessary.[12]

Changes in bowel patterns are a common concern for many older adults. As with digestion, many of these changes are the result of a decrease in activity level or an alteration in diet. A decrease in the level of activity may also result in a decrease in food intake and therefore, a decrease in bowel activity. Many people complain of constipation because their bowels are not as "regular" as they used to be, but this may not be an indication of constipation. It may be natural for someone with little physical activity and minimal food intake to go a day or two without a bowel movement.[13] This is not typically a concern as long as bowel movements are consistent and there is no abdominal pain or bloating.

Decreased fluid intake and a diet lacking in fiber can affect the consistency of bowel movements. Increased fluid intake, fiber supplements, and stool softeners can improve consistency and are generally a better solution than laxatives.[14]

Movement

Bones and joints provide the structural support for our bodies and therefore take the greatest amount of abuse over time. The older we get, the more wear and tear our bones and joints experience, which can lead to osteoarthritis—a common problem faced by older adults. Osteoarthritis is best treated by lifestyle changes that may include weight loss or light resistive and flexibility exercises. Medications may be necessary to help control pain.[15]

Appearance

The skin seems to reveal the most visible reminders of age. Our skin becomes drier as we grow older due to a decrease in the number of oil-producing glands. It becomes thinner and less smooth because of a natural fat loss. The effects of age on the skin can be reduced with a well-rounded diet, including adequate fluid intake and the use of good quality skin creams or lotions. Precautions against sun exposure, which if practiced when young will prevent additional skin problems, continue to be appropriate for older adults.[16]

Dementia

Some of the greatest challenges of caregiving relate to caring for a loved one with dementia. Dementia is a frequently misunderstood condition that is often equally feared by caregiver and loved one alike. The term *dementia* has Latin roots and means "deprived of mind." Dementia is a nonspecific condition, or a syndrome that consists of a collection of varied cognitive symptoms. These symptoms may include impairment of memory, attention span, language skills, and problem solving abilities. Dementia can be static or progressive but is not reversible. There are many types of dementia, the most prevalent and most noted being Alzheimer's disease.[17]

Statistics indicate that the number of elderly with some form of dementia is on the rise.[18] There are many opinions as to why this is the case, but no one really knows the reason. For you, the caregiver, the numbers are not likely to change the way you care for your loved one, but a basic understanding of dementia may.

It is worth noting that sometimes an elderly person will develop sudden confusion associated with another illness or for no apparent reason. Caregivers often become alarmed and worry that their loved one has developed dementia. But dementia does not typically develop rapidly without an apparent cause. The sudden onset of these symptoms usually results from an illness that stresses the body enough to produce the symptoms of dementia. For example, a bladder infection or a respiratory virus, which may otherwise go unnoticed, can cause confusion or other cognitive symptoms. This type of condition is known as *delirium*. The symptoms of delirium generally subside when the underlying illness is treated or has resolved.[19]

Most Common Types

Alzheimer's disease is the most common and arguably one of the most devastating forms of dementia. The disease causes microscopic changes within the brain that include an abnormal collection of protein, which can generally only be detected during an autopsy. Its exact cause remains unknown, and diagnosis is primarily based on clinical history. Therefore, diagnosis can vary somewhat from practitioner to practitioner. The abnormal proteins cause neurological signals in the brain to be misdirected or blocked, which results in the characteristic memory loss and cognitive changes. Alzheimer's disease is a progressive dementia and will eventually lead to death as vital areas of the brain are affected. The rate of progression is different for every person, with the time from diagnosis to death ranging from four to twenty years. Most people die from the complications resulting from Alzheimer's disease rather than the disease itself.[20]

Vascular dementia, also known as multi-infarct dementia, is the second–most-common type of dementia and includes a variety of conditions that cause damage to the brain in the form of vascular lesions. These lesions result from ischemia, or the interruption of blood flow to the affected area of the brain. Technically, it is a static dementia because each ischemic episode is a separate event, and the dementia is limited by the number of damaging events. Therefore, proper diagnosis of vascular dementia can help prevent further damage to the brain if the cause of the ischemia is known. Left undiagnosed or untreated, vascular dementia can be progressive in nature as ischemic events continue to occur.[21]

Lewy body dementia is caused by damage to the brain cells from microscopic deposits of protein called Lewy bodies. These deposits eventually destroy the cells, resulting in cognitive changes as well as physical symptoms similar to those found in Parkinson's disease. Early cognitive symptoms include difficulties with attention and alertness and may include visual hallucinations.[22] In its early stages, Lewy body dementia is often confused with Alzheimer's disease or other dementias and therefore may be misdiagnosed. Actual occurrence rates may therefore be underreported.[23] Lewy body dementia is rapidly progressive and terminal.[24]

Alcohol-induced dementia occurs in older adults who have abused alcohol for many years. Prolonged ingestion of alcohol leads to destruction of brain cells, which eventually results in cognitive impairment.[25] Progression is generally limited by the cessation of alcohol consumption.[26]

Treatment

Since dementia cannot be reversed, treatment is focused on preventing future damage in the case of static dementias and on delaying deterioration in progressive dementias.

An example of treatment for a person who has vascular dementia following a stroke would be the implementation of blood pressure control measures or anticoagulation therapy to prevent future strokes.[27] Similar appropriate preventive measures would be taken for any form of static dementia.

Treatment for progressive dementia is somewhat less specific and a bit more complicated. The goal for treatment is to manage associated symptoms and slow the rate of progression. Medications and environmental adjustments are examples of methods that can help in the management of symptoms such as aggression or depression. In considering treatments to slow the rate of progression, you might wonder how you can slow down something when you don't know how fast it is going in the first place. You would be right to wonder, because neither a standard nor measurable rate of progression has been established. Still, there are medications that have been approved and are prescribed for the purpose of slowing down progressive dementias. Some even suggest that limited recovery of memory or improved cognition is possible. While most caregivers are anxious to try anything that may help their loved one, I have witnessed disappointment from many because their expectations exceed the scope of these medications. The best way to determine the appropriateness of any treatment plan is to have a candid discussion with your loved one's healthcare practitioner. Together, everyone can make the right decision for the circumstances. A trial run is often a good way of determining the effectiveness of treatments. If the chosen method works for your loved one, even if it does not work for others, you'll probably want to continue that course of treatment. On the other hand, if a treatment plan fails to provide benefits to your loved one, regardless of what others may have experienced, you will want to discuss possible changes with the prescribing clinician. To the extent possible, your loved one should be included in these discussions.

Prevention

Remember that static dementias are primarily related to underlying health conditions or events. Therefore, the way to prevent static dementia is to prevent these causative conditions or events. Measures taken to maintain health throughout life, such as eating a balanced diet, exercising regularly, and getting sufficient rest are the best methods of preventing some of the common health conditions that may result in static dementia. Proper treatment of diagnosed medical conditions is also essential.

Research findings vary widely when it comes to prevention of progressive dementias. This is due, in part, to the fact that there are so many unanswered questions about their cause. But there are some preventive measures that show promising results in multiple studies. I will focus on three that are generally simple to implement. Like the three Rs of a basic education (reading, writing, and arithmetic), I like to refer to the three Ss of dementia prevention: sustenance, stimulation, and socialization. These three things seem to play a part in delaying impending dementia, and recent studies even suggest hints of improvement in memory and activity levels by following these three Ss for those already suffering from dementia.[28]

Sustenance

A well-balanced and nutritious diet is essential in maintaining good brain health. Meals may need to be adapted to meet the needs of your loved one, but they should be value packed. While prepackaged or fast foods may be quick and easy, they usually lack the nutritional value your loved one needs. Sometimes, age can lead to picky eating, in which case *something* is better than *nothing*. In these cases, try to include as many of the basic nutrients as possible. When a proper diet is combined with simple but regular exercise, the body will be equipped with the essentials for self-maintenance and repair. Regular exercise can consist of a planned exercise program or something as simple as walking to get the mail or helping to fold the laundry. With just a little effort, many everyday activities can be turned into a simple form of exercise. The real key is to assure that there are opportunities for your loved one to maintain or increase his or her level of activity.

Stimulation

Keeping the brain active is like exercising a muscle; the more it happens, the stronger it gets. But real mental exercise consists of more than mere activity or entertainment. Watching a movie or listening to music is certainly more stimulating that sitting in a quiet room, but real stimulation requires your loved one to be actively engaged. When new learning is occurring, the brain is stretched and exercised. This equates to better brain health and increases the chances of delaying the onset of dementia. New learning does not need to be anything complicated, such as learning a new language. Simple crosswords or other types of puzzles, trivia games, or dictating a story are all activities that can stimulate your loved one's brain. With a little creativity, you and your loved one can come up with the activities that best meet his or her needs and interests.

Socialization

Spending time in the company of others and interacting with them provides immeasurable benefits to brain health. Mental stimulation will be the natural result of conversation as your loved one experiences emotions and memories that need to be understood, sorted, and responded to. Opportunities are also provided to share with others, which can require deep thought. The need to maintain social skills provides yet another source of stimulation. But beyond all of these benefits, healthy interpersonal contact leads to better mental health in ways and for reasons that are not completely understood. Seeking appropriate social opportunities may provide positive benefits for both you and your loved one. For best results, your loved one should be encouraged to be involved in socially engaging activities with different people at least three times a week. Of course, timing and frequency of social stimulation should be arranged according to the desires and preferences of your loved one.

It is interesting to note that these same suggestions, if practiced in everyday life, would improve overall health for anyone, with or without the possibility of a future diagnosis of dementia. Implementation of these suggestions does not guarantee that your loved one will not get dementia, but since there is no real downside to these lifestyle choices, there is nothing to lose.

Any of these suggested practices can be implemented, even if your loved one has already been diagnosed or is showing signs of dementia. As you try any of these ideas with your loved one, especially if dementia is already present, be observant of his or her reaction and respond appropriately. An appropriate response from you does not include forcing the issue to the point of arguing. Such a disagreement may make your elderly loved one more determined and does little more than frustrate you.

Care Basics

Providing hands-on care for your loved one can be a daunting task. If you find yourself in the position of giving personal care to your loved one, you may feel unqualified. But providing personal care for someone isn't rocket science. A little direction and instruction are often the only qualifications you need. Certainly, you know which basic physical needs require your attention, and most of us have had some experience in assisting others with them. For most, this experience came from assisting a child. While the basics of providing care are the same for children and adults, there are some differences that need to be understood. It can be tempting to treat your adult loved one as you would treat a child; and admittedly, particularly when dementia is involved, he or she may sometimes act like one. But your loved one has years of life experience that make it inappropriate to treat him or her like a child. The elderly, especially those with dementia, may have childlike needs, but don't confuse these needs with childish behavior. You must respect life experience and always treat your loved one with dignity. This includes involving your loved one in his or her own care to the extent possible based on health and cognitive levels.

Activities of Daily Living

You may have heard professionally trained caregivers speak about ADLs and wondered what they were talking about. ADLs, or *activities of daily living*, refer to the things we do in a normal day and include personal care and hygiene as well as work and leisure activities. For the elderly adult, ADLs generally consist of tasks that caregivers most commonly assist with. These tasks usually include cleaning teeth, combing hair, shaving, dressing, bathing, eating, taking medications, and using the restroom. For some, tasks relating to things such as hearing aids, eyeglasses, dentures, or anti-embolism stockings may also be part of routine ADLs. Your loved one's ADLs are those things you assist him or her with on a daily basis to maintain cleanliness, comfort, and health.

There is no magic formula for assisting your loved one with ADLs. Unless your loved one is confined to bed or is immobile, his or her daily routines may not be much different from your own. But be warned; the response to your help may not be quite what you expect. As discussed earlier, while some elderly adults appreciate help with their ADLs, others may be resistant, even when they know they could use the assistance. This can be frustrating for you, the caregiver. Unfortunately, his or her resistance and your frustration do not eliminate the need for your help. The means to success in these situations are patience and understanding. If you patiently try to determine the reason for the resistance, you have a good chance of being able to overcome the objections. Some reasons for declining your help may be as simple as not liking the order in which you are attempting to do things, or perhaps it is simple embarrassment about

It is never appropriate to talk about loved ones in their presence as though they are not there.

requiring help with a very personal need. Things that may not seem like a big deal to you can be important to your loved one. Don't argue or try to talk your loved one out of his or her feelings. If a requested way of doing things does not interfere with or prevent you from providing the needed assistance, then do it as requested. Also, recognize that there is a difference between care that *should* be provided and care that *must* be provided. Occasionally, you may need to put off nonessential care in order to avoid upsetting your loved one and starting an argument. For example, even though it is the social norm to bathe or shower daily, there are times when this could be considered nonessential care. Because the process can be taxing or upsetting for some elderly, there may be days when your loved one is too tired, or for some other reason will not cooperate with your efforts to help with a bath or shower. In many cases, skipping a shower, or even setting up an every-other-day bath schedule, would benefit your loved one more than a daily fight through the process. Certainly there are times, as in the case of an incontinent loved one, when daily showering or bathing would be essential.

Caregivers sometimes cause resistance to needed care by unknowingly and unintentionally disregarding their loved one's dignity. This occurs when personal or embarrassing information about your loved one is shared in his or her presence. There may be times when you find yourself discussing your loved one's needs, and perhaps your frustrations, with others. While conversations of this nature can be appropriate if the intent is to improve care, they should never occur in the presence of your loved one unless he or she is an active part of the discussion. Caregivers should exercise extreme caution where such conversations are concerned, and should not get caught in the trap of believing that poor hearing, dementia, sleep, or distance prevent your loved one from hearing or understanding what you are saying. It is never appropriate to talk about loved ones in their presence as though they are not there.

Caring for a loved one who is confined to bed or is immobile does have additional challenges. These caregivers become good at putting clothing on one side of the body at a time and rolling or leaning their loved one from side to side. Detailed explanations of how to provide care in these circumstances are beyond the scope of this book, and the need for such explanations may indicate that you should seek help from someone experienced in this type of care. Do not think that turning to someone else for their expertise means that you have given up. Since the purpose is to learn the techniques for providing ADLs in a safe manner for both you and your loved one, this extra help may only need to be temporary.

Sharing Their Reality

One of the greatest temptations for caregivers is to always make sure their loved one has a firm grip on reality. Many older adults have moments of confusion about where they are, whom they are with or what day it is. When this happens, it is usually okay to reorient them to the here and now, especially if they ask for your input. If your loved one has dementia, confusion may be a constant or near constant state for him or her. In this situation, attempts at reorientation usually lead to frustration for both of you. You are not likely to convince your loved one who is stuck in the 1950s that Elvis is no longer King. While this may be a poor example because many of you caregivers may be stuck in the same time warp as far as Elvis is concerned, it may help you relate to how easy it is to share in your loved one's reality. In most cases, it makes no difference in your loved one's care if they think "Blue Suede Shoes" is still at the top of the charts. Some caregivers feel that correcting their loved one will aid in memory retention. In cases of "senior moments" when confusion is occasional and temporary, correcting may help. But when dementia is involved, correcting your loved one usually leads to an argument. Frequent arguments of this nature can lead to your loved one resisting care or not trusting you as a caregiver.

Acknowledging

Many caregivers have learned not to question their loved one's alternate reality, but some still have a difficult time knowing how to deal with it. For example, it would be difficult to share in a reality that includes memories of mistreatment that you know never occurred. In situations like this, many caregivers simply ignore or dismiss their loved one's perception of reality. But even if these memories are incorrect, they still exist for your loved one, and so do the emotions associated with them. Remember, perception is reality and ignoring your loved one's emotions is, in effect, ignoring them as a person. Dismissing your loved one's concerns is equal to saying that he or she isn't important. As you avoid accepting something you know to be a misperception, you may also discover that you are failing to acknowledge your loved one's emotions. It is possible to acknowledge your loved one's concerns without accepting the memories as fact, and it is to everyone's benefit to do so. In reference to the previous example, you don't have to agree that a previous caregiver used to leave him or her alone for days on end, but you can acknowledge that being left unattended would be frightening. There is almost always common ground with any reality or situation on which you and your loved one can agree. Find the common ground, and always acknowledge your loved one's emotions and concerns.

Therapeutic Pretense

Sometimes, actively participating in your loved one's reality and acknowledging his or her emotions may require you to tell an untruth in order to avoid confrontation. Many people worry about "lying" to their loved one. This was something that I struggled with, even as a professional caregiver. But I have come to understand that saying something untrue to someone who is confused is not lying as long as the motives are pure.

Here is how I see it. Saying something untrue to your loved one for your personal gain would constitute lying. Likewise, speaking an untruth that is harmful to someone and benefits no one would also be considered lying. On the other hand, if you tell your loved one something that you know is not completely true but do so for their benefit or protection and at no expense to anyone, you are showing wisdom and kindness and using what I call "therapeutic pretense." An example may be telling your loved one that the juice you gave him or her for breakfast tasted different because it was a new brand, though you know it was because it contained the vital medication he or she refused to take earlier. Therapeutic pretense is nothing more than treating emotional, physical, and spiritual needs with the use of comforting and supportive words.

Whether dealing with an elderly loved one or in everyday life, there are times when the absolute truth does no good but leads to harm. In these cases, say those things that are best for the situation. I don't mean to suggest that you can stretch the truth anytime with regard to your loved one's care. There may be times when lying seems the easiest way to deal with a situation, but it is not the right way. Anything built on a foundation of lies will eventually collapse. My personal belief is that the truth should always be told unless doing so causes harm, and an untruth should never be told except to prevent harm.

Maintaining Your Health

With the exception of the actual care given, the most important thing you can provide for your loved one is a healthy caregiver. Too often, caregivers become so completely engrossed in the care of their loved one that they neglect their own well-

Full-time caregivers need to recognize that a real break from each other is often healthy for both you and your loved one.

being and develop health problems themselves. This results in two people needing assistance and creates greater stress for everyone involved in the care. It is vital that you pay attention to your own physical, mental, and spiritual needs. Stress comes with caregiving, but wise planning can minimize stress. Do your best to maintain all of the healthy lifestyle habits you had before you became a caregiver.

If you had an exercise routine before caring for your loved one, you may need to adjust it, but don't abandon it. If you did not exercise before, you may find that your stress will decrease and your energy level will increase with regular enjoyable physical exercise. Just remember, a little exercise is better than no exercise, so find something you enjoy and do it as often and as regularly as you can.

A proper diet will help you maintain sufficient energy to deal with the added stress. Try to eat well-balanced meals and to eat regularly. Cheating may be an occasional necessity, but don't cheat too often. When you do cheat, don't allow any resulting guilt to add to your stress.

It can be difficult to take time for yourself, but most caregivers can find a way. Even if you can't get away, often you can do relaxing things with your loved one. Enjoy games, movies, reading, or other activities together if you can. Full-time caregivers need to recognize that a real break from each other is often healthy for both you and your loved one. Even if it is just long enough for a haircut or to do a little grocery shopping, time away can give you new energy and a refreshed attitude. Arrange with a trusted neighbor, family member, or even a professional caregiver to give you an occasional break.

Socialization is as important for you as it is for your loved one. You don't have to get away to socialize. A visit with a common friend can provide respite for both of you, so don't be afraid to invite your friends over for a visit. This kind of break can be good for everyone.

Though you may share common feelings and beliefs with your loved one and others around you, there is a level of spirituality that is deeply personal. Know what and how you believe and then foster that belief. Assisting someone else with their needs is one of the best ways to discover and strengthen that inner personal spirituality.

NOTES

1. R. F. Wilson, N. T. Aggarwal, L. L. Barnes, C. F. Mendes de Leon, L. E. Hebert, and D. A. Evans, "Cognitive Decline in Incident Alzheimer Disease in a Community Population," *Neurology* 74, no. 12 (2010): 956–64.

2. Carol A. Miller, "Vision," *Nursing for Wellness In Older Adults*, 5th ed. (Philadelphia, PA: Wolters Kluwer Health/Lippincott Williams & Watkins, 2009), 337–61.

3. Lillian Sholtis Brunner et al., "Assessment and Management of Patients With Eye and Vision Disorders," *In Textbook of Medical-Surgical Nursing*, 12th ed. (Philadelphia, PA: Wolters Kluwer Health/Lippincott Williams & Watkins, 2010), 1756-1800.

4. T. V. Caprio and T. F. Williams, "Comprehensive Geriatric Assessment" *Practice of Geriatrics,* 4th ed., ed. E. H. Duthie, P. R. Katz and M. L. Malone (Philadelphia, PA: Saunders, 2007), 41–52.

5. Stefanie L. Russell and Jonathan A. Ship, "Normal Oral Mucosal, Dental, Periodontal, and Alveolar Bone Changes Associated with Aging," *Improving Oral Health for the Elderly: An Interdisciplinary Approach,* ed. Ira B. Lamster and Mary E. Northridge (New York City: Springer, 2008), 233–46.

6. Dana L. Wolf and Panos N. Papapanou, "The Relationship Between Periodontal Disease and Systemic Disease in the Elderly," *Improving Oral Health for the Elderly: An Interdisciplinary Approach,* ed. Ira B, Lamster and Mary E. Northridge (New York City: Springer, 2008), 247–72.

7. N. Salles, "Basic Mechanisms of the Aging Gastrointestinal Tract" *Digestive Disease* 25, no. 2 (2007): 112–17.

8. Susan S. Shiffman, "Taste and Smell Losses in Normal Aging and Disease," *Journal of the American Medical Association* 278, no. 16 (1997): 1357–62.

9. Alberto Pilotto et al., "Clinical Features of Reflux Esophagitis in Older People: A Study of 840 Consecutive Patients," *Journal of the American Geriatrics Society* 54, no. 10 (2006): 1537–42.

10. Peter J. Kahrilas, Nicholas J. Shaheen, and Michael F. Vaezi, "American Gastroenterological Association Medical Position Statement on the Management of

Gastrointestinal Reflux," *Gastroenterology* 135, no. 4 (2008): 1383–91.

11. Barry D. Weiss, "Diagnostic Evaluation of Urinary Incontinence in Geriatric Patients," *American Family Physician* 11, no. 57 (1998): 2675–84, 2688–90.

12. Randall H. Neal and Drew Keister, "What's best for your patient with BPH?" *The Journal of Family Practice* 58, no. 5 (2009): 241–47.

13. Giancalo Spinzi et al., "Constipation in the Elderly: Management Strategies," *Drugs and Aging* 26, no. 6 (2009): 469–74.

14. Ibid.

15. Nisha J. Manek and Nancy E. Lane., "Osteoarthritis: Current Concepts in Diagnosis and Management," *American Family Physician* 6, no. 61 (2000): 1795–1806.

16. Marcia Ramos-e-Silva and Coelho DaSilva Carneiro, "Elderly skin and its rejuvenation: products and procedures for aging skin," *Journal of Cosmetic Dermatology* 6, no. 1 (2007): 40–50.

17. Mayo Clinic, "Dementia," last modified November 22, 2014, http://www.mayoclinic.com/health/dementia/DS01131.

18. Cleusa P. Ferri et al., "Global prevalence of dementia: a Delphi consensus study," *Lancet* 366, no. 9503 (2006): 2112–17.

19. John Barton, "Dementia and Delirium," *Johns Hopkins Medicine*, accessed February 15, 2014, http://www.hopkinsmedicine.org/gec/series/dementia.html.

20. Alzheimer's Association, "What is Alzheimer's?" accessed February 15, 2014, http://www.alz.org/alzheimers_disease_what_is_alzheimers.asp.

21. Alzheimer's Association, "Vascular Dementia," accessed February 15, 2014, http://www.alz.org/alzheimers_disease_vascular_dementia.asp.

22. Alzheimer's Association, "Dementia with Lewy Bodies," accessed February 15, 2014, http://www.alz.org/alzheimers_disease_dementia_with_lewy_bodies.asp.

23. Lewy Body Dementia Association, "What Is LBD?" accessed February 15, 2014, http://www.lbda.org/category/3437/what-is-lbd.htm.

24. Lewy Body Dementia Association, "Diagnosis," accessed February 15, 2014, http://www.lbda.org/content/diagnosis.

25. Sushma Gupta and James Warren, "Alcohol-related dementia: a 21st Century silent epidemic?" *British Journal of Psychiatry* 193, no. 434 (2008): 351–53.

26. David W. Oslin and Mark S. Cary, "Alcohol-Related Dementia: Validation of Diagnostic Criteria" *Journal of American Geriatric Psychiatry* 11, no. 4 (2003): 441–47.

27. Laura E. Middleton, "Promising Strategies for Preventing Dementia," *Dementia Treatments and Developments*, ed. Patrick McNamara (Santa Barbara, CA: ABC-CLIO, 2011), 75–98.

28. Ibid.

Part 2

"He who chooses the beginning of the road chooses the place
it leads to. It is the means that determines the end."[1]
—Harry Emerson Fosdick

RELIEF DRIVERS

O n any long journey, it is crucial that the driver be alert and aware of his or her surroundings. Changing road conditions, surrounding traffic, and even the passengers can affect the drive. On some journeys you may be the only driver, while on others, you may have help. Sometimes you may be the backup driver. In any case, in order to assure the safety and comfort of the passengers, it is vital that the most qualified driver for the current conditions is behind the wheel.

As a caregiver, you may find yourself "in the driver's seat," or you may be the relief driver. In some cases, you may have the opportunity to be both, depending on current needs. For proper care for your loved one, make sure that the right people are filling the proper roles. Care needs will change, making it necessary at times to adjust caregiving roles. Never forget that your loved one is part of the care team and should, as able, be involved in making decisions about his or her care needs. The chapters in this section focus on providing or selecting the right kind of help for your loved one once care needs are established.

Chapter four addresses care provided at home and the available resources for in-home care. Chapter five examines the needs that require care sources outside of the home and how to select the right sources. Chapter six explores the unexpected difficulty but definite necessity of allowing others to provide care when you are not the primary caregiver.

NOTES

1. Henry Fosdick, *Living Under Tension: Sermons on Christianity Today* (New York: Harper & Brothers, 1941), 111.

Chapter 4

CLOSE TO HOME

DETERMINING THE BEST WAY TO DELIVER CARE AT HOME

M*arian was worried when it grew dark outside and there was still no sign of Bert. He had gone for his usual evening walk but should have returned long ago. She was about to get in the car and go look for him when there was a knock at the door. Marian was both relieved and distressed to see a police officer and Bert standing on the front porch.*

"Is this your husband, ma'am?" the officer asked.

Marian just nodded.

"I picked him up about a mile from here. He seems fine, but he's a little confused." The officer helped Bert into the house and handed Marian Bert's wallet. "You may want to keep him close to home," the officer suggested as he left.

Marian didn't know what to think. Bert didn't even seem concerned, but he was definitely confused. What caused this sudden, strange behavior?

She wanted to be shocked by this experience, yet somehow Marian knew in the back of her mind that she was almost expecting it. For months, she had been ignoring, perhaps denying, some of Bert's behaviors; they were nothing big, just little things that seemed odd at the time but were easily dismissed. The more she thought about it, the more she realized there was a problem. She couldn't remember the last time Bert made proper change at the grocery store. And why had he stopped writing checks and begun using the credit card for everything? Even at work, his secretary mentioned that Bert had been giving her more and more responsibilities that had previously been his.

It took several visits to the doctor and even more tests, but Bert was diagnosed with early-onset Alzheimer's, a condition that usually strikes early and moves fast. Bert didn't understand the diagnosis when it came, but Marian did. She knew that her life was about to change.

There were lots of tears when she was alone, but Marian tried to be positive around Bert. Though they had a supportive family, none of them lived nearby. Their children helped resolve financial and other issues, but the bulk of Bert's care would be up to Marian.

At first, Bert was easy to care for. Sure, there was the need for some adjustment, but for the most part, things were pretty routine. In time, it became more difficult for Marian to help Bert keep himself occupied during the day. He would become restless and then sometimes a little aggressive. Marian attended an Alzheimer's support group and learned from other caregivers that there were resources available. She and Bert visited a local senior day-care center that someone recommended. Bert seemed to enjoy his time there, and with a little persuasion and creativity, Marian was able to get him to go each day.

When Bert's condition progressed to the point that he could no longer leave home, Marian utilized the help of a local home health agency. They were able to come in several times a week and help bathe and dress Bert and would even take him for a walk when he felt up to it. As his condition declined, Bert was eventually placed on hospice care. Hospice personnel assisted Marian in meeting Bert's continuing needs as well as providing support for her through this difficult time. Following Bert's death a few months later, the hospice agency provided follow-up support for Marian. She was grateful for the help of so many people who really cared about Bert and made a difficult time much easier to deal with.

Family and Friends

One of the greatest fears among the elderly is being moved to an "old-folks home" as soon as they begin requiring a little extra help. As discussed earlier, this fear, coupled with the fact that many even make their children promise that they will never move them from their house, commonly leads to conflicting feelings for caregivers. But often your loved one can have all of his or her needs met at home (at least during the early stages of care). There may be other family members or friends who are available to provide assistance. Sometimes, all it takes to find those willing to help is simply to ask.

While it is usually best to have one person oversee all aspects of care, many people can and may need to be involved in actually providing the care. Most of the focus up to this point in the book has been on personal care needs, but there are other aspects of caring for a loved one. Managing finances, making medical and other appointments, preparing meals, and housekeeping are just a few of the additional items that may need to be attended

1. If someone is overworked, they need help.

2. If someone fails to carry out their assigned responsibility, they need to be replaced.

to but do not need to be handled by one person. Examine your circumstances and then divide the responsibility for care among all willing and able family members and friends if it makes sense to do so. In some situations, only one or two caregivers may be needed. In other circumstances, several people may need to be involved. Determining the right number of caregivers and their specific responsibilities does not need to be a difficult task. There are two basic things to consider when making care assignments: availability and a basic knowledge or a real desire to learn about the assigned responsibility. In addition, applying two simple rules will assure that proper care is provided:

1. If someone is overworked, they need help.

2. If someone fails to carry out their assigned responsibility, they need to be replaced.

Even more important than these basics is genuine concern for the one receiving care.

Paid Caregivers

If there are no family members or friends available to assist in providing care for your loved one, you may consider hiring someone to provide care in the home. Most communities have access to agencies that provide personal care at home. While this option would not be the most economical if around-the-clock care is needed, it can be an affordable way to meet occasional or part-time needs.

Some families hire individuals to provide care assistance for their loved one. These caregivers may be retired and seeking a little additional income or may be students who appreciate the opportunity to earn a little money. Classified ads and college job boards can be a good way of finding this type of help, but word of mouth is generally the most effective means of learning about these individuals. Finding caregivers in this way can be a good option depending on the level of care needed by your loved one and the experience level of the hired caregiver. Always do your homework and actively check references to assure that your loved one will be safe and well cared for.

Adult Day Care

Many communities have licensed adult day-care centers that are equipped to meet the basic care needs of your loved one during daytime hours. The day-care setting can be helpful for families who primarily need assistance during working hours and whose loved one does not require extensive care. Whether utilized on a daily basis or just for an occasional need, adult day care can make it possible to keep your loved one at home for longer.

Home Health and Hospice

Most insurance companies have a home health benefit available to those who qualify. To qualify, your loved one would typically require the assistance of a registered nurse or licensed therapist on an intermittent basis. Those who qualify for home health are usually able to have the additional assistance of a home health aide to assist in ADLs several times a week. Home health is generally a temporary service but can be a beneficial bridge during a difficult time, such as after a fall, following a hospitalization, or during an illness. If you feel that your loved one may benefit from home health services, speak with his or her physician or contact a home health agency for more information. An online search for *home health services* will provide information on agencies in your area. If you know someone who has used home health for him- or herself or a loved one, you may consider asking what agency was used and the services provided were satisfactory. Though a physician's order is needed for home health services, any agency can help you in obtaining the required orders.

Hospice care is another benefit covered by most major insurers and can be a valuable source of care assistance as loved ones near the end of life. In addition to providing assistance with the care of your loved one, hospice also offers emotional support for everyone involved in care. In most cases, to qualify for hospice, your loved one must be in the advancing stages of his or her illness and within six months of death as determined by a physician. As with home health, your questions about hospice can be addressed by speaking to your loved one's physician, contacting a hospice agency directly, or asking an acquaintance who has had experience with hospice.

Temporary Care

Multiple changes in care needs in a short period of time or numerous changes in health status can be overwhelming for some dependent older adults. This can lead to increased irritability and resistance to care that, unless resolved, may compromise his or her overall health or safety. If you have concerns of this nature for your loved one, you may want to speak to his or her primary care practitioner about seeking help through a senior behavioral health program. Gerontological Mental Health or Geriatric Psychiatry programs, commonly referred to as gero-psych or geri-psych programs, consist of a short-term in-patient stay in a psychiatric hospital or hospital psychiatric unit with specialized training in care of the elderly. The hospital stay is usually less than two weeks long and focuses on providing seniors with the coping skills to deal with the changes they have experienced, and it usually includes behavioral stabilization and medication regulation.

Respite care refers to temporary short-term relief for caregivers. It can provide an opportunity for full-time caregivers to have a break while assuring that aging loved ones continue to receive the care they need. Caregivers can arrange respite for as short as one day to as long as several weeks. Many private care, home health, or hospice agencies offer short-term respite in the home. Longer-term respite may be available from assisted living communities or skilled nursing facilities. In many areas of the country, state and local governments offer respite resources for caregivers. Though regulations for respite vary from state to state, services are generally available in most areas, and specific information can be obtained from local providers.

Community Resources

Within most communities are untapped resources that aid in caring for the elderly. These services may range from daily meal delivery to counseling services. The federal government as well as each state has a department on aging, which includes community resources for the aging and their caregivers. Information about these services can be found in the Government section of your local telephone directory or on the Internet by searching for *aging services* on your state or county's website.

Local senior centers may not be able to directly assist in the care of your loved one, but most provide opportunities for a break. Meals and entertainment are usually offered on a regular basis, so you may consider occasional visits to the local senior center if your circumstances allow. Some centers provide transportation to their scheduled events as well as other organized outings. Health fairs, fitness events, or other activities that may benefit your loved one are often a part of the annual calendar for many senior centers. In addition to providing a change of scenery, these events can be a valuable source of socialization for your loved one and may even prove to be a source for networking with others in similar situations to yours. Contact your local senior center to find out what it may have to offer your loved one.

Churches often offer assistance with an aging loved one. While most are not set up to assume a major role in caring for the elderly, they can supplement the care given by others. If your loved one is part of a church congregation, you may want to discuss his or her needs with the congregation leader. Even if that person does not have the means to assist with caregiving, these leaders and other members of the congregation are usually excellent sources of spiritual and emotional support. You will probably find many people within the church who have been or are caregivers and who would be happy to share their knowledge with you.

Chapter 5

VENTURING OUT

SELECTING THE
RIGHT "OUTSIDE" HELP

M avis was in good health in spite of a recent heart problem. The new medication she was prescribed didn't seem to have any negative side effects and didn't slow her down. Though her physician did advise her to be careful about overdoing things, he said it would be okay for her to continue to participate in all the activities she enjoyed. She was particularly grateful that she was still allowed to drive.

Occasionally, Mavis would have an episode with her heart that left her a little tired and unsettled. Generally, a little rest was all she needed to feel better. Over time, these episodes increased in frequency and duration. The doctor had told her that the day would come when she would need to have a pacemaker implanted in order to control the episodes.

As she considered the fact that her children all lived in different states, Mavis realized that if she were to have a problem and was unable to call for help, she would be in trouble. She began to look at options. Her children recommended that she move close to one of them, but she liked where she lived. She considered a senior-living condominium but didn't see that moving there would be much different than living at home. There was a nice retirement community where one of her friends lived, but Mavis felt she still wanted a little more assurance. Finally, she settled on an assisted living community not far from her current home. Though she really didn't need any assistance yet, she knew at some point she would and didn't see the need to make two moves.

It didn't take long for Mavis to settle in to her new surroundings. Her apartment was spacious, the staff and other residents were friendly, the activities were enjoyable, and the food was delicious. Admittedly, there were times when she wondered if she had been a little premature in moving from her home, but she was happy.

After nearly a year in the assisted living community, Mavis collapsed in the dining room. Staff members responded immediately, and Mavis was transported to the hospital, where a pacemaker was implanted. Her physician told her that the quick action of the staff had saved her life. She was grateful for her earlier decision to move to where she had assistance available.

Independent-Living Communities

Concerns about safety are frequently the driving force behind a move from home to an independent-living community, sometimes referred to as a retirement community. These communities are primarily designed for seniors who are able to live on their own, but will benefit from the security and convenience of community living. Independent-living communities differ in type and in the services or amenities available; therefore, the benefits they offer your loved one will also vary.

Some communities provide personal condominiums within a campus or neighborhood. Each condominium has its own outside entrance, allowing for greater privacy but making it necessary for residents to go outside to access other areas of the community. Residents may have their own kitchen and be able to prepare their own meals if they choose to do so, or they may have the option of joining other residents in a common dining area.

Other independent-living communities are designed more like a hotel, with individual apartments accessed through a common lobby, thus eliminating the need for residents to go outside when visiting other areas of the community. Apartments typically have a refrigerator or small kitchenette but may not be designed for meal preparation. Meals are often provided in a common dining room.

Residents in independent-living communities may be monitored on a regular basis but do not receive personal assistance with ADLs from community staff. There is often a daily program of activities for residents to participate in. Beauty salons, barbershops, and laundry facilities are typically available to residents within the community. Some communities have fitness and recreational areas. Amenities such as linen service, meal delivery, or transportation may also be available at some communities. Because personal assistance is not offered by independent-living communities, they are not regulated by local, state, or federal agencies.

If your loved one is in need of assistance with ADLs, an independent-living community may not be the best choice for him or her. If your loved one needs only limited assistance and you are confident that those needs are not likely to increase in the near future, independent living may still be appropriate. In these cases, personal assistance can be arranged through a home health or other caregiver agency.

Assisted-Living Communities

Assisted-living communities offer a combination of housing, health-care, and personal services in an environment that promotes independence for those who are no longer able to remain at home. Assisted-living communities provide assistance with personal care and are therefore licensed and regulated by the state. Most provide private apartments that may include a kitchenette but are not generally designed for meal preparation. Meals are served in a common dining room, and residents are encouraged to join with other residents at mealtime. A daily activity program is provided for residents. In addition to personal care and meal preparation, amenities and services can include such things as linen or laundry service, transportation, a fitness center, housekeeping services, and a beauty salon and barbershop.

Residents in assisted-living communities are monitored closely by community staff. Assistance with personal care can range from reminders to hands-on assistance, depending on your loved one's needs. Assistance with ADLs is typically available, though regulations regarding medication assistance vary from state to state. Most assisted-living communities contract with or employ a registered nurse who is available for medical monitoring, but this also varies according to individual state regulations.

Though most seniors desire to remain at home, circumstances often prevent home from being the best choice. Assisted living is an excellent alternative because residents can continue to do many things for themselves yet have help available as needed.

Skilled Nursing Facilities

Skilled nursing facilities or nursing homes are for those who need around-the-clock care from nurses and nursing assistants. Skilled nursing facilities also have in-house licensed physical, occupational, and speech therapists. Those requiring skilled nursing generally need services beyond what can be offered in assisted living.

Facilities are licensed and regulated by the state and can provide personal services including medication administration.

Admission to a skilled nursing facility can be on a short-term basis, such as when recovering from an illness or when therapy is needed following surgery. Long-term admissions result when a condition or illness progresses to the point that no other care setting is able to meet the individual's personal and medical care needs.

Continuing Care Retirement Communities

Another option that is available in many areas is a continuing care retirement community, which offers independent living, assisted living, and skilled nursing all on one campus. Those living in a continuing care retirement community are able to have their care needs met as they progress, without having to move to another community. A continuing care retirement community can be a good option for a couple when each needs a different level of care. In considering this option for your loved one, be sure to visit each area of the campus, even those that you may not be considering at the time, to be sure that all levels of care offered meet your desired standard.

Memory Care

Many assisted living and skilled nursing facilities provide memory care units for residents with dementia or other memory impairments. These units are typically secure so no one can enter or exit without a special code or the accompaniment of a facility staff member. Staff members on memory care units are specially trained to meet the additional needs of those with impaired memories.

Residential Hospice

A residential hospice is a freestanding facility that offers the same services as in-home hospice with the added benefit of around-the-clock care from hospice staff. If your loved one qualifies for hospice care, you may want to explore this option to see if it is the right choice for him or her.

Residential hospices are not available in all areas.

Chapter 6

NO BACKSEAT DRIVING

ALLOWING OTHERS TO CARE FOR YOUR LOVED ONE

Coleen had been a good mother, and Vicki wanted nothing but the best for her. So when Coleen began showing symptoms of dementia and was no longer safe to live alone, Vicki brought Mom home. It wasn't too bad at first, but providing personal care to an adult was something new for Vicki. After a conversation with her mother's doctor about a minor fall Coleen had experienced, Vicki contacted a home health agency that was able to arrange for a physical therapist and a home health aide to visit several times a week. The therapist was doing a good job, but it seemed that he always wanted to come when it was inconvenient, and the aide assigned to help Coleen with her showers just couldn't seem to get it right. Vicki decided it wasn't working out like she had hoped, so she discontinued the services.

After a few months, Vicki found that Coleen's need for constant supervision was interfering with her family responsibilities. Coleen was too disruptive to go with her to her children's activities, so Vicki usually missed them. She knew she had to make other arrangements for her mother. She was uncomfortable having someone else in her home when she was out, so decided that a personal care service was not an option. Then Vicki found a small assisted-living facility in town, and after a tour and visit with the staff, she decided she would give it a try. Coleen moved in without too much protest. Vicki quickly determined that she needed to visit her mother more than once a day because Coleen wasn't receiving the kind of care she deserved. During a conversation with the administrator of the *facility, Vicki learned that her mother could be a bit disruptive during activities and had even threatened other residents and staff. The administrator asked Vicki if she had any suggestions that might help the staff keep Coleen calm. Vicki had no suggestions and figured it was probably just staff incompetence. She was tempted to take her mother back home right then but decided to give the staff a little more time to work out their issues. Then the administrator called to tell Vicki that Coleen had walked away from the facility and crossed a busy highway. Fortunately, the staff had noticed she was missing, and within a few minutes had Coleen safely back with the other residents, but the administrator informed Vicki that this was not the first time Coleen had attempted to leave the facility. Since Coleen had successfully made it across the street, the administrator said she could not guarantee Coleen's safety and Vicki would need to move her to a secure facility.*

Vicki was secretly glad she'd been asked to move Coleen, because she wasn't particularly happy with the care her mother was getting, and Vicki was actually away from her family more than if she'd kept Coleen at home. Besides, she'd found another facility she really liked and although they wanted to admit Coleen to their locked unit, Vicki convinced them that the previous wandering episode had been a misunderstanding. So Coleen was admitted on a trial basis. But Vicki found the same problems with the new facility. It only took three months for Vicki to move Mom back home.

This time, Vicki knew how to handle the situation. She'd worked out things with the family and . . . it was only a week before Coleen wandered away from home and had to be brought back by the police.

Vicki found a secure dementia unit as part of a skilled nursing facility in another county that she felt could meet her mother's needs. Of course, once Coleen moved in, this facility proved to be no more competent in the eyes of Vicki than the other places had been. But this facility was so far away from home that she just couldn't spend much time with her mother. So she reluctantly left Coleen's care in the hands of the staff.

It was several weeks before Vicki was able to arrange time to visit her mother, but when she did, she found Coleen well cared for and relatively settled. This time, Vicki just sat back and watched. Soon she noticed that the staff here treated Coleen the same as the staff at the other facilities; only this time it was okay, because something had changed. There had been no change in the care, but there had been a change in Vicki's perspective.

Accepting Help

Recognizing the need for additional help in caring for your loved one is one thing; actually arranging for and allowing someone else to help can be another thing altogether. Sometimes, even after recognizing the need for assistance, a caregiver may find it difficult to accept help with their loved one. While there are many rea-

The ultimate care is provided by caregivers whose lives are properly balanced.

sons for this type of reaction, including guilt and a need for control, I believe the most common reason is a genuine desire to assure the best care for your loved one. This is especially true if your loved one is unable to give input into the decision-making process due to dementia or other factors.

As discussed previously, unchecked guilt can lead to a lack of appropriate care for your loved one. In a similar way, the desire to be in complete control of your own life as a caregiver can lead to overcontrolling your loved one's care. Overcontrolling caregivers feel that no one else is capable of providing adequate care for their loved ones, and they typically find themselves overworked and frustrated while actually leaving their loved ones' care lacking. If you feel guilty about requiring help or feel that you are the only one qualified to meet your loved one's needs, then you may need to step back and consider if you are doing what is in the best interest of your loved one. It can be difficult to see these tendencies in yourself, so pay attention to what those around you are saying. Be willing to listen and seriously consider what you hear.

It is natural to feel that no one cares about your dependent loved one as much as you do, and this naturally leads to the logic that since you care the most, you just need to buckle down and do what needs to be done for them. I agree with this vein of logic as long as you realize that doing the right thing might involve actually including others in your loved one's care. Of course you want the best for them, and when you're at your best, you probably are the best caregiver. But how often are any of us at our best for any length of time? Consider how much is going on in your life outside of caring for your loved one. If you just said to yourself, "I have no life outside of this," then you probably need to consider sharing some of the caregiving responsibility rather than shouldering it alone. The ultimate care is provided by caregivers whose lives are properly balanced. This often requires a team effort. Besides you and your loved one when possible, the team may be made up of family members, friends, or professionals either at home or elsewhere. As you determine where your strengths are in meeting your loved one's needs, concentrate your care in that area. Let those who have expertise in other areas assume care where they can. This approach allows you time for other aspects of life and helps you focus your strengths where they can most benefit your loved one. Even if you are the primary caregiver or the one designated as the final decision maker, you can remain in charge and provide the best possible care for your loved one by maximizing all of your resources.

Choose Well

When obtaining help for your loved one from anyone, make sure you choose the right help. This includes not only the right level of care but also the right quality of care. Whether you are employing a care agency to provide assistance at home or are selecting a facility, do your homework. Don't be afraid to ask for references from potential caregivers. Tour facilities you may be considering, and take note of whether or not the residents there look happy and well cared for. Do staff members look happy? Are there any odors that concern you? Most people have acquaintances that have been involved in caregiving or know someone who has, so ask around. Make sure to involve your loved one in the process to the extent possible. Most importantly, trust your "gut feeling."

It Is Their Job

Once someone you trust has been chosen to assist in caring for your loved one, don't stand in that person's way. Certainly you want the best care, but there are usually several equally good methods of achieving that care. A trained caregiver may not do things your way, but that doesn't make the caregiver's methods wrong. Too often, well-meaning informal caregivers insist that the trained caregivers do everything in a specific way because that's the way they've always done it. Of course, these informal caregivers never consider that the way they've "always done it" may be the reason they now need help doing it. Trained caregivers often employ equally caring yet more efficient and safer methods to do things than people who, perhaps like you, have assumed the role of caregiver. This is not to say that all trained caregivers are better than you. But unless they are actually harming your loved one in some way, give them a chance.

You may find that they really do know what they are doing and their methods, though different, are fine. And don't forget your loved one's input. Even if he or she is unable to tell you, your loved one's reactions to the caregiver will provide valuable insight into the information you need.

It is not easy to share your loved one with someone else in this way, because no matter how caring that person is, he or she doesn't feel the same about your loved one as you do. You should continue to be involved with your loved one's care at whatever level you are able. Work closely with a trained caregiver, and be supportive in their efforts. It has been my experience that as you work together, you will usually find that even paid caregivers have a genuine desire to give your loved one the best care possible.

Realistic Expectations

Caregivers and family members occasionally get caught in the trap of believing that their loved one's condition changes once they are receiving professional assistance. Of course, this is not the case. Your loved one will continue to have the same needs no matter who cares for them, and trained caregivers are likely to face the same problems you struggled with. Their formal training may make it possible for them to avert some challenges you faced or handle difficult situations more effectively than you were able to. This does not necessarily mean that they are smarter or better than you, but they are able to approach your loved one's care without a history that may include frustration or anger aimed at you by your loved one. Allowing someone else, someone new, to deal with common challenges may even allow you to improve your relationship with your loved one.

Occasionally, someone you employ to care for your loved one, whether at home or in a facility, will not meet your expectations. If this results in actual harm to your loved one, then immediate action should be taken to remedy the situation; otherwise, don't be hasty in making major changes. Remember, no caregiver, including you, is perfect, so don't expect perfection from trained caregivers. They will make mistakes. Things will not always go as planned. One way of judging the quality of the caregiver or facility is to observe their response when a mistake occurs, or something goes wrong. Reputable and qualified caregivers will do all they can to correct the situation and take steps to prevent a repeat.

Don't assume anything when employing a caregiver or moving your loved one to another care setting. Ask all the questions up front and read the fine print. If a situation arises in which you remember something differently than they do regarding your loved one and his or her care arrangements, be willing to review your admission documents and other paperwork before assuming you're right. Many times, I have watched family members embarrass themselves by insisting they were correct regarding a matter, only to find that the paperwork bearing their signature proved otherwise. When you remember how stressful it was to make the arrangements in the first place, you'll likely admit that you may have been told things you have forgotten. Gather all the facts before you accuse someone of being dishonest, deceptive, or uncaring. Your loved one will receive better care if you cooperate with those assisting you in providing it rather than if you make the caregivers feel as though they are constantly under scrutiny from you. If you find that there is substandard care or that you or your loved one has somehow been misled, take the steps necessary to correct the situation and assure proper care for your loved one.

Your expectations for your loved one's care should be high, but try not to make them unrealistic. While it's true that keeping your loved one clean, well fed, and safe is just the minimum standard of care, these are things that can usually be built upon. Remember why this particular type or level of care was chosen, then realize that there may be some "little things" that just don't get done at first. Honestly consider how important these things are before you upset your loved one with another change or move, then work with the caregivers and give them a chance to do those things that really matter to you and your loved one. Again, the key is to choose well and let those you've chosen do their job. You should expect the best, but don't expect miracles; they may happen, and if they do, you can be grateful. If your expectations are reasonable and you honestly feel your loved one's needs can be better met with other arrangements, then you should certainly do what you and your loved one feel is right.

Complete Awareness

If at any time you suspect that your loved one is being neglected or harmed in any way, take immediate action to correct the situation. Though it is important to let trained caregivers do their job, it is also important that you be completely aware of what to expect from them and what kind of care they are providing to your loved one. Laws against abuse and neglect can only protect your loved one if the offending caregiver is reported.

Bear in mind that abuse and neglect of the elderly is a serious offense and therefore should be reported accurately. A false or incorrect accusation could ruin someone's career or damage the reputation of a care facility. Be careful about automatically assuming that a bruise or other minor injury was the result of abusive care to your loved one, but always ask questions. If the answers you receive seem suspicious, report your concerns to a superior of the one you suspect. If for some reason you have concerns about the organization that employs your loved one's caregiver, then report your concerns to the proper authorities. Every state has an abuse hotline or equivalent that allows you to anonymously report suspected neglect or abuse. In the event of extreme cases, you can report your concerns to local law enforcement.

Part 3

"He that can have patience
can have what he will."[1]
—Benjamin Franklin

ROUGH ROAD AHEAD

There may be times during an extended journey when you encounter unexpected behavior from travel companions. Most of us have experience with the driver who takes a wrong turn but refuses to admit the error until it's obvious that there is no other option. Perhaps you've traveled with someone who feels their experience makes it unnecessary to accept the advice of others who may be more knowledgeable. Possibly most difficult is the journey that finds everyone in the vehicle bickering over differences of opinion about which restaurant to stop at, how many rest stops are needed (or whether they are needed at all), and how fast the car should be going. Ultimately, the one in the driver's seat has the power to make the final decision, but that doesn't mean others will agree or comply without complaint, and that can make the journey miserable for everyone.

Like drivers on a long road trip, caregivers must be prepared for those difficulties that are part of life, but seem amplified by the stresses of caregiving. These annoyances can grow into major problems that distract you from your role as caregiver. The chapters in this section help you prepare to face these difficult situations and overcome them without major disruptions in your loved one's care.

Chapter seven addresses the issue of denial, which can potentially surface in any aspect of caregiving. Chapter eight examines your loved one's understandable desire to retain his or her independence and how to balance that desire with appropriate care. Chapter nine tackles the difficulty of dealing with differences of opinion between those involved in your loved one's care.

NOTES

1. Benjamin Franklin, *Poor Richard's Almanack* (Waterloo, IA: The U.S.C. Publishing Co., 1914), 29.

Chapter 7

"IT'S NOT MY FAULT. I JUST TURNED WHERE YOU TOLD ME TO"

RECOGNIZING DENIAL AND MISPLACED OR INAPPROPRIATE BLAME

Dora was confident that she would come through once again. She had never let anything stop her. When her husband died, she got a job to support her young family. She couldn't afford a car, so Dora walked or rode her bicycle to make deliveries. After a heart attack, she was only away from work for a few days, much to her doctor's dismay. Her first stroke slowed her down slightly, but she exercised on her own long after therapy had finished until she regained her full strength. A more recent stroke, however, did seem to take a little more out of her. It left her paralyzed on one side, and she had difficulty swallowing and speaking. The doctors told Dora that she would probably regain her full ability to speak and eat, but they were less hopeful that she would ever regain control of her right side.

"They just don't know me," Dora declared to her children. "Nothing has stopped me before. Why should this be any different?"

Dora worked hard in rehab. After a few weeks, she had completely regained her ability to safely swallow, and while her voice wasn't quite as strong or clear as it was before the stroke, everyone was pleased with how well she could speak. But the weakness in her right side persisted, making it impossible for her to walk without assistance. She hated depending on others, but in her current state, she had no choice.

After several more weeks of therapy, and no improvement in her strength, it was time for Dora to be discharged from rehab. She told her family that *she was almost as strong as she had been before the stroke. Her family was anxious to see how she could do on her own, but the therapists and discharge planners insisted that Dora needed more help than she could receive at home. Reluctantly Dora agreed to be discharged to an assisted living facility.*

It didn't take Dora long to settle into her new living arrangements, though she was still determined that she would one day move back home. She was convinced that her only problem was that they didn't work her hard enough at the rehab facility.

Though her family had arranged for personal services at the assisted living facility, Dora refused most of the help. She felt that it would help her become stronger and more independent if she did things on her own. Unfortunately, in her attempts to be independent, Dora often found herself on the floor. As the number of falls increased, the staff found themselves in Dora's room more frequently. They felt that instead of becoming stronger, Dora seemed to be getting weaker, but she insisted they were wrong. Eventually, Dora earned an overnight stay in the hospital. While in the hospital, tests revealed that the effects of Dora's heart attack many years earlier now left her heart extremely weak. The doctors informed the family that it was only a matter of time before Dora's heart would fail completely, so they recommended that she go back to assisted living and "take it easy" for her remaining months.

Dora did return to assisted living, but she told her family, "I'm not going to take the easy way out." She was determined that hard work was all she needed to become stronger, and no amount of arguing with her family or anyone else could change her mind. Dora passed away the following day while attempting to exercise her legs.

No One Is Immune

You, your loved one, other caregivers, friends, and family members are all capable of experiencing denial. Denial comes in many forms. Whether it's your loved one denying the need for additional help, a family member denying that your loved one is terminally ill, or another caregiver denying that a wound is getting worse, it is denial all the same. Denial is a natural defense mechanism, but when unbridled, it has a destructive nature that impedes progress. In caregiving, that equates to undermining your loved one's care by shifting the focus from reality.

Dealing with your own denial is difficult. It requires that you have an open mind and are willing to listen to and consider the opinion of others. Turning personal denial to acceptance is within your control. But dealing with the denial of others can seem impossible. It is true that you have no control over the way others think or feel, but you can *influence* their thoughts and feelings. In all cases, the worst response to someone's denial is arguing with him or her. Once arguing begins, all listening stops. You are much more likely to persuade someone toward reality through a discussion of opinions than a battle of wills. It is, however, important that you accept the reality that there may be times when denial cannot be overcome. In these cases, unless your loved one or their care is being negatively impacted, it may be best to just let everyone believe what they choose to believe.

When it is your loved one who is exhibiting signs of denial, the methods of helping him or her accept reality are no different than they would be for anyone else, but it can be more difficult than dealing with an extended family member or casual caregiver. When those in need of care or assistance are unable to accept the reality of that need, it may be tempting to force them into reality. As discussed previously, forcing leads to resistance, so any attempt on your part to force your loved one to accept care or a different perspective will only lead to greater resistance to those things. Except in cases where there are legitimate concerns for health or safety, it is always best to discuss things with your loved one, find common ground, and—as necessary—negotiate a workable resolution. This may require willingness on the part of all caregivers to ease into the needed care as long as your loved one is not facing a serious health or safety risk.

Not So Different

When it comes to advancing age or declining health, we all would like to think that our situation is different. Since we are all individuals, there are differences in all circumstances, but there are also similarities. Age and its associated conditions may not follow an exact pattern, but they do follow a pattern—one that most are unable to escape. Your loved one could fall, illnesses may occur, disorders typically progress, deterioration usually happens, and life will eventually end for everyone.

Having a positive attitude about life's circumstance is crucial, but so is reality. It has long been accepted that optimistic people have better overall health and faster recovery times after illness than do those who tend to be pessimists. But no amount of positive thinking will cure dementia or restore damaged organs. This is not to say that you can't believe in miracles.

But because miracles aren't within your control, don't neglect necessary care or treatment for your loved one while you're waiting for one to occur.

When we receive information about a loved one's condition that includes both good and bad news, most of us try to focus on the good. While this is a healthy approach for everyone, it can become unhealthy if we block out, ignore, or deny the bad. Most of us as caregivers are neither immediate nor conscious deniers. Denial usually happens gradually, without awareness, as we concentrate on positive advances and forget about the possibility of anything negative happening. When something negative does happen, our automatic response tends to be denial. For some people, denial can be a natural defense mechanism. But just like grief, denial can become unhealthy if it persists. Failure to work through persistent denial can progress to feelings of anger and blame.

While most people try to focus on the positive, be aware that denial of positive things is also a possibility. Some people have a negative disposition that makes it difficult to accept good news or admit times of positive progress. Regardless of the source, perspective or reasoning behind it, denial must be recognized as such so that it can be appropriately managed and overcome.

Bad Things Happen

It seems that our society has become one of denial. Look at how many people fail to recognize that past experiences can help prepare them for future outcomes. As a result, they forge ahead with little attempt to prepare for what lies in front of them and are then surprised by what occurs. If the occurrence is unpleasant, they become angry and look for someone to blame, when in reality, the blame lies with them. It is almost as if these people assume that nothing negative happens in life unless someone else has done something wrong. A common example of this is people who persist in making unhealthy choices in spite of all the evidence that they are shortening their lives. They become ill and then want to sue someone for making the choices available to them.

In caregiving, just as in life, undesirable things happen. When something bad happens, you may find yourself in crisis mode. It is at this point that you must focus on the care needs that accompany the crisis rather than the reason for the crisis. Once your loved one's needs are met, then you can go back and look at the cause. If the crisis resulted from something that needs to be changed, then take the necessary steps to assure that the change happens. If something needs to be reported to someone, then report it to the appropriate person. Your time will be better spent and your loved one better cared for if your focus is on learning what you can from a situation rather than trying to decide who should be blamed for it. Remember that a common risk of pointing fingers is that you will reveal to others the dirt under your own fingernails.

I have observed over the years that most often, blaming is preceded by anger. Situations involving the care of your loved one may arise that result in you or others becoming angry. Few good decisions are made when they are made in anger. Things tend to be said and accusations made before all circumstances are known or understood. Caregivers often react to a comment from their loved one without confirming the story or considering important factors, such as the fact that their loved one has dementia or often becomes confused when upset. Even in the absence of dementia or known episodes of confusion, memories have been known to fade with advancing age. Impaired hearing or eyesight can also affect how circumstances are viewed or remembered. Wise caregivers or friends and family of the loved one will take the time to get the facts straight before angrily reacting to a situation and making a decision they may later regret.

I am not suggesting that you should always discount everything your loved one reports to you. He or she may very well be sharing something that is completely truthful, but it is also possible that what is being remembered is not quite the way things are and is always from their perspective. Even with no consideration for age, four different people sitting around a table and looking at a tissue box will, if asked, only be able to describe the box from their perspective. Each of the four may give true but different descriptions. Only when all four descriptions are considered can you come up with a completely accurate image of the box. So it is in dealing with negative reports from or about your loved one. Always listen to everyone involved, and then consider all the facts before responding to any negative situation.

Crisis prevention is a better option than disaster cleanup. If you have concerns that you feel need to be addressed with a physician, a paid caregiver, or even another informal caregiver, deal with them right away. Seemingly small things, like a slightly elevated temperature, a sudden change in behavior, or a feeling that something is wrong all warrant further investigation. It is difficult to always know when to wait and when to act on these or similar things, but it is always better to err on the side of caution. If you aren't sure whether to say something, you probably should.

Chapter 8

REDUCED SPEED AHEAD

BALANCING YOUR LOVED ONE'S INDEPENDENCE WITH APPROPRIATE CARE

At age eighty-seven, Jed had a perfect driving record. It had been over thirty years since he'd been cited for a traffic violation. His last accident was ten years ago, and it really didn't count because he'd just fallen asleep at the wheel. At least, that was Jed and his wife Della's perspective. Their family, however, saw things differently. In fact, it had reached the point that no one in the family, except Della, would ride in a car with Jed driving.

The family got together and agreed that Jed was no longer safe to drive. He had told them many times that when he no longer felt safe driving, he would give up his license. The biggest problem was Della. She was afraid of being stuck at home if she and Jed had to rely on the children for transportation. Anytime anyone said anything about Jed's driving, she always defended him. "He's a good driver and has never had an accident," she would say. Reminders about past accidents did little good.

Because they knew how important the trips to the post office and grocery store were for their parents, Jed and Della's children were reluctant to do anything. In a family meeting, they determined that they needed to figure out how to accomplish the task with the least amount of disruption to their parents. They agreed to meet again the following week and make a plan.

Two nights before the meeting, there was a report on the evening news about an elderly gentleman who had lost control of his car and driven onto a playground full of children. One child died and several were seriously injured.

One of Jed and Della's sons knew the time was right. The next morning, he visited his parents and showed them the morning paper. The front page told of the terrible tragedy from the previous afternoon. The son then expressed his desire to prevent anything of that nature from happening to his father. Jed was upset by the article, but Della immediately began talking about Jed's driving record as she remembered it. The son turned from his mother and kindly but firmly told Jed he felt it was time to give up his license. For the next hour, the three talked. Della's argument never changed. Wisely, the son focused on his father. He and Jed had a heartfelt discussion about the situation. The son was careful not to get upset or argue at any point during the conversation. When his mother interrupted, he simply smiled and then returned to speaking with his father. In the end, Jed agreed to stop driving. Della still complained.

The following morning, everyone was grateful for their brother and his willingness to do what no one else wanted to do. Everyone agreed that the right thing had been done, and a schedule was set up between family members to provide daily transportation for their parents. All of the children understood the need to acknowledge their mother's complaints, but to remain firm in the fact that their father would no longer be driving.

It's Hard for Them Too

It is because of our basic human nature that most of us desire to remain as independent as possible for as long as possible. This desire is a good thing and is possibly one of the reasons the limits of life expectancy continue to be challenged. But it is that same human nature that can, at times, cloud our perception of personal abilities as we age. Caregivers frequently become frustrated when their loved one is "too stubborn" to accept help or "too bullheaded" to consider another point of view. Yes, they are set in their ways, but for them, the issue is more likely about independence than anything else.

How would you respond if someone told you that from now on, they will be helping you get dressed in the morning, or beginning tomorrow, they will have control of your bank account? As I have stressed previously, limiting your loved one's independence should only be done

Even when health and or safety are a concern, your loved one should be involved, to the extent possible, in any discussion that may result in a loss of independence for them.

when health or safety are at stake. Every attempt should be made to allow your loved one to remain as independent as possible for as long possible. Even when health and or safety are a concern, your loved one should be involved, to the extent possible, in any discussion that may result in a loss of independence for them. When such a decision must be made, with or without your loved one's approval, do not forget that you are taking something away from a mature adult. Parents often punish a child by taking away a privilege, so it should come as no surprise to you that your loved one may experience the same feelings as a punished child and may resist your efforts. As caregivers, we must never lose sight of how our loved ones must feel each time we provide help with something they believe they are still capable of doing on their own. There is no way around the fact that they probably won't like it any more than you would.

Care-*full* Negotiating

You may wonder how to overcome this sense of loss or punishment. In reality, unless your loved one accepts the change and recognizes it as necessary, you really can't; but you can usually work within it. Even if your loved one disagrees with a decision or action, there is a good chance you can negotiate with him or her if it is understood why you are doing what you are doing. For example, you arrange for someone to prepare meals for your mother who has been losing weight, because she is skipping meals. She understands that she is losing weight, but insists that she is able to prepare her own food. You promise her that if she can gain ten pounds and keep it on for a month, you will *discuss* letting her prepare her own meals again. Keep in mind that other things could change in the meantime, so be careful about making a promise you may not be able to keep, and never make a promise if you have no intention of honoring it. Allowing your loved one to progress toward a goal gives him or her hope in the future. If dementia is a factor, you can still help your loved one set goals, even if you know they are unlikely to be achieved. You may need to occasionally remind your loved one that he or she is working toward greater independence, thus providing them with continued motivation and boosted confidence.

I have seen a tendency among caregivers to attempt to ban loved ones from certain activities. This usually leads to resistance from your loved one because a ban basically equates to you simply trying to force the issue. Rather than insisting that your grandmother not use the stove for cooking because she has started two dishtowels on fire in the past week, create a situation where she doesn't need to cook. Help her plan a menu that includes breakfast and lunch items that do not require her to use the stove, and then arrange for a hot dinner to be brought in to her. If she is able to use a microwave, perhaps someone could spend one day each month helping her make meals that can be kept in the freezer and warmed in the microwave at her leisure.

For loved ones who don't understand that you are trying to protect them from harm, especially when dementia is involved, you may need to recruit the help of others and perhaps employ the use of therapeutic pretense. If your father's driver's license needs to be renewed, and you know that his continued driving would pose a danger to him and others, you can tell him he needs his doctor's approval for the renewal. A simple conversation with a cooperative doctor can assure the needed approval will not be given. This and similar methods should never be used as a matter of convenience or simply to get your way. They should only be employed in cases where health and safety would otherwise be at risk.

As you negotiate with your loved one, be careful not to set up your own failure. Even if you are dealing with a loved one who has dementia, being too specific or too detailed may get you into trouble. Open deadlines and generalities give you some needed wiggle room. An example would be a woman who insists she does not need to be in an assisted living facility in spite of the fact that she can't safely walk from her bedroom to her bathroom without assistance. A wise caregiver may tell her that when she is able to walk one hundred feet without assistance, then you will *discuss* the possibility of returning home. Words must be carefully chosen so you don't end up breaking a promise and destroying trust between you and your loved one. Phrases such as "we'll discuss it" or "then we'll look at it again" help accommodate changing circumstances and allow for continued negotiations if needed.

Chapter 9

"I THINK YOU SHOULD CHANGE LANES"

DEALING WITH DIFFERENCES OF OPINION

D*an was shocked by the phone call from his younger brother John. He was calling from the emergency room. Their ninety-three-year-old father, Ralph, had collapsed while visiting John's family. He had been rushed to the hospital by ambulance. John told Dan that it didn't look good for their father.*

When Dan arrived at the hospital, the doctor met with him and John in the waiting room outside of the ER. He explained that there was some bleeding in Ralph's brain that had caused him to collapse. Surgery was possible, but because of the location of the hemorrhage and their father's age, surgery was risky. The doctor said a decision needed to be made quickly.

"So if he has the surgery, he'll be all right?" John asked.

"If everything goes well in surgery, then it's possible, but there is no guarantee."

"And if he doesn't have the surgery?" Dan asked.

"There's a good chance he will die, or . . . ," the doctor hesitated.

"Or what?" Dan questioned.

"Well, at the current rate of progress, he will be lucky to survive the night, but there are things we can do that might slow down the bleeding, and it's possible that it could even stop," the doctor said.

"Then why risk the surgery?" Dan asked.

"The chances are greater that we can slow the bleeding if we operate," the doctor answered.

"So his chances are better with the surgery?" John asked hopefully.

The doctor was slow to respond. "It's a delicate surgery. There's a chance he wouldn't even make it from the operating room."

"It sounds like you're telling us that he has no chance, no matter what we decide," Dan said.

"Unfortunately, we don't have any definitive answers," the doctor began. "Either way, if he survives, it is likely that he will have some serious problems. He may not be able to walk or do anything for himself, and there's the possibility that he won't be able to speak."

"Then tell us this," Dan said, "Is there any chance, either way, that our father will come through this without major problems?"

The doctor sighed. "He collapsed because of pressure on the brain. Some of that pressure is from the bleeding and some is from resulting inflammation. So there is a small possibility that if the bleeding is stopped and the inflammation goes down, he won't have all of those problems. Just don't get your hopes up." He looked at the brothers sympathetically and walked toward the door, then stopped and turned around. "I'll leave you two to talk about it for a minute. I'm right outside if you have any questions."

"We have to do the surgery," John insisted when the doctor had closed the door.

"But, John, what are we doing to him if he can't walk or talk or—well—do anything? What kind of life is that?"

"You're assuming the surgery won't be successful. We have to try," John said.

"You heard what the doctor said. He might die in surgery, and if he survives, has he really survived?" Dan argued.

"His chances are better with the surgery," John insisted.

Dan shook his head. "His chances are poor no matter what. Look, I love Dad just as much as you do, but we'd be torturing him to make him go through a major surgery and then leave him totally incapacitated. I say we don't do anything and see what happens. If he's supposed to live, he will. If he's not, he won't."

"So you just want to stand here and let him die?"

"I want what's best for him," Dan said. "He's lived a good life. Maybe it's his time to go."

"And maybe it's not!" John responded. "Maybe he won't make it through

surgery, but maybe he will. Maybe he will be incapacitated, but maybe he won't. We have to let them do the surgery."

"I really think surgery is more of a death sentence than doing nothing," Dan said.

John shook his head. "I disagree. I think that we need to do something, and then what happens, happens."

"And I'm suggesting that we do nothing and accept what happens."

"Don't you think doing something—anything—is better than doing nothing?" John asked.

"Usually," Dan said, "but I'm not sure that's the case this time."

"Dan, I couldn't live with myself if I went through the rest of my life knowing we had a chance to help Dad and did nothing about it."

Dan looked at the ground and shook his head again. "John, I'm not sure I agree with you, but I do see your point. I don't want to lose a father and a brother." He turned, opened the door and invited the doctor back in. "Doctor," he said, "we want you to do the surgery."

Ralph did survive the surgery and underwent two months of rehabilitation afterward. He was able to walk with assistance and even feed himself. Though it was difficult to understand what he was saying, he could talk. Ralph lived for three more years, and both of his sons accepted the outcome of the decision.

Opposing Family Views

Opinions are formed based on a variety of factors. While it is common for members of a family to have similar opinions about most things, differences are not uncommon. Individual personalities and experiences influence how opinions are developed. So when family members have a difficult decision to make, each one approaches it from his or her own perspective and therefore forms an opinion. Remember from the tissue box example in chapter seven that each opinion, though different, is valid and is part of an accurate broader perspective.

Differing opinions do not have to be a bad thing. If viewed as an opportunity to further explore all possibilities from a wider viewpoint, differences can be enlightening and help family members make more informed decisions. Family members need to listen to each other, and everyone's opinion needs to be considered.

Family members that have their minds made up and are unwilling to listen to or consider anyone else's opinion can be the cause of delaying appropriate care for a loved one. Often, care decisions are not made until everyone agrees. This approach is preferred and helps promote family unity during a difficult time. But making a decision based on majority opinion may be necessary if total agreement is not achieved in sufficient time to prevent any suffering by your loved one.

A designated decision maker will be crucial in preventing unnecessary delays in your loved one's care in the event that appropriate discussion fails to lead to consensus among family members. As discussed earlier, the designated decision maker must carefully weigh all options, and then make a decision based on all available information and genuine concern for your loved one.

Out-of-Towners

One common source of differing opinions is family and others who have genuine concern for your loved one but who are not directly involved with his or her care on a routine basis. These people often come from out of town to visit your common loved one and discover that his or her condition has declined. Too often, these visitors fail to consider the natural deterioration that occurs with time and age and instead blame you or other caregivers. They often want to dictate how care should be provided, even though they may be unaware of your loved one's specific needs.

If you ever find yourself as one of these out-of-towners, recognize that the changes you see in your loved one would likely have occurred even if you had remained right at their side. If you, as a caregiver, encounter one of these visitors, try to calmly assure them that your loved one is being appropriately cared for, but more importantly, continue to give appropriate care. The quality of care you oversee or deliver will ultimately speak for itself.

The best way to avoid this out-of-towner reaction is to regularly communicate with family members and others who have a genuine interest in your loved one and who are likely to visit. Frequent updates about what is happening in your loved one's life will remove much of the shock that is sometimes experienced by an infrequent visitor. Modern methods of communication such as e-mail, social networking, and blogs make this type of communication easier and may prove to be well worth the investment of time required to assure frequent updates.

Others' Opinions

Everyone has an opinion, and most are willing to share it. Nearly everyone you come into contact with knows or has been a caregiver and therefore may feel qualified to give advice or share his or her opinion. There is nothing wrong with a general interest in you and your loved one, and it's okay to listen to what he or she wants to share. But as discussed earlier, take that person's opinion for what it is: an opinion. It may be helpful to you or your loved one and it may not, but it is usually beneficial to look at every situation from as many qualified perspectives as possible.

Sometimes, it is tempting to view the opinions of a professional as always correct. While physicians, nurses, therapists, trained caregivers and others may have experience to back up their opinion, it is still only an opinion. Certainly, their opinions should weigh more heavily on a care decision for your loved one than your uncle's cousin's daughter-in-law's neighbor's opinion. Be careful that you don't confuse an opinion expressed by someone you consider a professional with a professional recommendation. It can be difficult to tell the difference between an opinion and a recommendation, so if you are unsure which is being offered, simply ask. I don't mean to suggest that you should always question the opinions of professionals, but too often, I have witnessed caregivers make a decision they feel uneasy about because of something a professional told them. If you feel uneasy or have questions about anything you are told by any professional, ask additional questions until you feel good about the answer, or ask another professional for another opinion. Then make your decisions based on what seems best for your loved one.

If you feel uneasy or have questions about anything you are told by any professional, ask additional questions until you feel good about the answer, or ask another professional for another opinion.

Part 4

"What seems to us as bitter trials are
often blessings in disguise."[1]
—Oscar Wilde

ENJOYING THE
JOURNEY

Have you ever been traveling along, enjoying the scenery, and sudden realize you passed your turn-off—about thirty miles ago? What about pulling over to change a flat tire and then removing all the luggage from the trunk to access the spare only to discover that it is also flat? Can you imagine the disappointment when you have planned to stop at the side of the road to enjoy a picnic lunch but get caught in a torrential downpour that just won't seem to end? It seems that long journeys are just bound to have setbacks.

Problems and setbacks are part of every aspect of life, and you'll find that there are no exceptions in caregiving. Unplanned and undesirable circumstances will arise in spite of all your efforts. There are two choices when it comes to dealing with adverse situations: you can face them with a positive attitude or you can face them with a negative attitude; but you must face them. The chapters in this section offer suggestions for making the best of any situation.

Chapter ten addresses preparations that will help you face unforeseen situations. Chapter eleven explores the value of humor in caregiving. Chapter twelve offers ways to focus on the good times.

NOTES

1. Oscar Wilde, *Epigrams of Oscar Wilde*, Wordsworth Reference (Ware, UK: Wordsworth Editions, 2007), 128.

Chapter 10

"I THINK THIS IS OUR EXIT"

PREPARING FOR THE UNKNOWN

Lorraine was excited about the additional help available for her mother in the assisted living community. Anita's dementia had made her a bit defiant. Lorraine knew that her mother's condition had moved beyond her ability to care for Anita at home.

Anita settled into the assisted living setting quickly. She liked her apartment, the food, the staff, and especially the male residents. Most of the time, Anita was cooperative with the staff in allowing them to provide the personal care she needed. Lorraine felt good about the move and was grateful that her mother was doing so well.

For several years, there was little change in Anita's condition. Lorraine visited her mother almost every day. She would help with her laundry or take her for a walk. Lorraine often joined Anita for a meal, where her mother would introduce her to her latest unsuspecting male friend. Lorraine loved her mother and was thankful that she was so happy.

Occasionally Lorraine would come to visit when a staff member was helping Anita. She could tell that the staff really cared about her mother as they lovingly assisted Anita in getting ready for her day or helped her with other personal needs, even when Anita resisted the help.

Though she had always been energetic, Anita began slowing down shortly after her ninety-eighth birthday. She showed less interest in activities, her appetite was decreased, and she even quit flirting with the men at her dining room table. Soon, she was unable to leave her room. Plans were made to move Anita to a skilled nursing facility where her increasing needs could be appropriately met.

The day before Anita moved, Judy, a young staff member and newly certified nursing assistant, stopped Lorraine in the hall. "I just love your mother," she said. "It's hard seeing her decline like this."

"Thank you," Lorraine said, "and I agree, it is kind of hard."

"I just finished my training last month, so I've never had a resident leave before," Judy said.

"This is a first for me too," Lorraine said. "In fact, in spite of knowing this day would probably come, I've spent the last few years hoping it never would. Mom loves it here, and I hate to move her."

"I wish they'd let her stay," Judy responded.

"I used to wish the same thing," Lorraine confessed.

"Used to," Judy questioned. "What do mean?"

Lorraine motioned for Judy to join her on the sofa at the end of the hall. "Well," Lorraine began as she sat down, "when Martha, the director, called me to set up a meeting, I knew what it was about. I cried myself to sleep that night. When I was driving to the meeting the next morning, I went through all the reasons I was going to give Martha to convince her that Mom shouldn't move. Mom loves the other residents and they love her, the staff is like family, and—I was saving the best for last—the move will kill her."

"I guess that didn't work," Judy said.

"I didn't even use it," Lorraine admitted. "By the time I arrived, I realized I was being selfish. I wanted all the things for Mom that would keep me happy, but I knew they weren't in Mom's best interest. Even though most of my arguments were true, I knew Mom needed more help in her remaining days than she can safely get here. You can see that, can't you?"

Judy nodded. "I guess."

"Mom probably doesn't have much time left, so I need to be sure every day is the best it can be for her," Lorraine said.

"I don't like thinking about that," Judy said.

"Well," Lorraine suggested, "just think about how you've been a part of Mom's happiness."

Judy smiled. "I can do that," she said.

Expect the Future

Sometimes we have control over the events we'll face in the future and sometimes we do not, but we always have control over whether or

If your view of aging and death differs from your loved one's, you will need to learn about his or her view in order to provide proper care and support as a caregiver.

not we make an effort to be prepared for them. We can't be equally prepared for all future events because often we don't know specifically what the future holds for us, but by picking up this book, you demonstrated that you are willing to be proactive about what is ahead.

We will all face challenges in life, we will all age, and we will all die. Though we know these events are coming, we don't always know the details. Without some extreme intervention, the challenges we will face, how old we will get, and when and how we will die are mostly out of our control. But that doesn't mean we can't prepare for them. Most of us have been taught to have a little money in savings for use in an unexpected emergency. That same principle can be applied to preparations for advancing age, declining health, and eventual death.

As a caregiver, you know in the broad sense what the future holds for your loved one. General preparations will help both you and your loved one face these challenges as they come. Take the necessary steps to be mentally, physically, and spiritually prepared for the future.

Understanding Values

The set of values and beliefs you possess dictate your behavior and make up your value system. It is important that you understand both your own value system and that of your loved one. If your view of aging and death differs from your loved one's, you will need to learn about his or her view in order to provide proper care and support as a caregiver. Be careful not to project your own views on your loved one or to think less of him or her because of values that differ from yours.

Certain beliefs and views are part of a particular generation; others are common to families or communities. Most people who associate closely will share some common values. As a caregiver, you will most likely find that you have many beliefs in common with your loved one, especially if you are related. Whether related or not, making a point of knowing which values you share with your loved one and focusing on them will strengthen your relationship. While it is important to understand your differences, it is equally important not to dwell on them.

Caregiving leaves no room for value judgments. Your disapproval of a particular value held by your loved one will not change it, nor should it prevent you from providing needed care. As a nurse, there have been many times that I have cared for someone whose values led to choices that created the need for the care I was providing. While it would have been easy for me to make judgments about a patient who had smoked all of his life and was dying from lung cancer, it would have been inappropriate to do so. As a caregiver, the focus must be on providing needed care, not on the reasons any particular form of care is needed.

I recall a time when members of two opposing gangs were brought to the emergency room where I was working. Both of them needed treatment of injuries sustained in a fight with each other. I could have refused to provide care for their senseless injuries, but I knew that it was the individuals I was treating, not the wounds. Similarly, I have known people who have been abandoned by a loved one as a child, only to be placed in the position of either caring for that same loved one many years later or arranging for appropriate care when there was no one else that was willing or able to do so. While individual and family circumstances vary, the need to be prepared to care for elderly loved ones is almost universal.

Chapter 11

"AT LEAST THERE'S A SPARE—ISN'T THERE?"

LAUGHING WHEN IT'S NECESSARY AND SOMETIMES WHEN IT'S NOT

F red walked into the administrator's office and dropped a paper on his desk. "Get on your thing and fix that," he demanded.

Troy picked up the paper to discover it was a traffic citation. "Fix it?"

"Yeah, I want you to get on your thing there and fix it," he repeated, pointing at Troy's computer.

Troy held back a chuckle. "Well, Fred, I'm afraid I'm not able to do that."

"Why not? You've got one of them things just like down at the courthouse, don't ya?"

"Yes, I do," Troy admitted. "But mine is designed to do different things. I'm afraid you're going to have to go to the courthouse to get this taken care of."

"You're useless," Fred muttered as he snatched the citation out of Troy's hand and stormed out of the office.

Sharon could hardly wait to see her mother. She was taking her to the dance at the senior center. They'd spent the entire day shopping for just the right outfit. New shoes with a matching handbag and a hat completed the ensemble. The dress Ivy wanted was a little more expensive than Sharon had hoped to spend, especially since she'd probably only wear it once. But Sharon knew this was a special night for her mother, so she decided to spend the extra money.

Ivy came out of the bedroom wearing her new outfit and holding a pair of scissors in her hand. "What do you think?" she asked.

Sharon gasped, "Mother, what happened to your dress?"

Ivy smiled. "It covered up my new shoes, so I shortened it."

Sharon started to cry, then to laugh. After all, she knew the dress probably wouldn't be worn again anyway. "It's lovely, Mom, but maybe I could help you straighten the hem a little," she suggested.

They were delayed slightly while Sharon removed Ivy's jagged work, and repaired the hem. They both enjoyed the evening, and Ivy received plenty of compliments . . . on her shoes.

Uncle Phil's smile was wide, and Jenny could feel his excitement as he climbed into her car. Usually he was waiting inside the lobby at the retirement center when she picked him up, but today he was standing on the curb. Phil was joining her family for Christmas.

At home, Jenny and Ron got Phil settled into the guest bedroom downstairs. Phil took a nap until dinnertime and then joined the family for a wonderful Christmas Eve feast. After dinner, Phil played with the children until it was time for them to go to bed.

"You be sure and get me up when the kids are awake," Phil insisted as Ron helped him down the stairs and into his bedroom.

"It'll be early," Ron said.

"I don't care," Phil insisted. "I want to watch them open their gifts."

"Okay," Ron promised. "I'll come get you as soon as they're awake."

Early Christmas morning, the children's screaming woke Jenny and Ron. Jenny calmed the children in the family room while Ron went downstairs to get Phil.

After a few minutes, Ron came up the stairs alone.

"Where's Uncle Phil?" Jenny asked.

Ron shook his head. "I don't know. He wasn't in his room."

"Did you check the bathroom?" she asked.

Ron nodded. "He wasn't there."

"Well, that's crazy," Jenny said. "Where could he be? He can't get up the stairs on his own."

"You're right. He has to be downstairs somewhere," Ron said.

"You wait here kids. Mommy and Daddy will be right back," Jenny said.

Ron and Jenny went downstairs and searched Phil's room. They looked in the bedroom closet and even under the bed. Phil was not in the bathroom, the laundry room, or the storage room.

"I can't imagine where he could be," Ron said.

"Uncle Phil!" Jenny yelled.

"Uncle Phil!" Ron repeated.

Somewhere in the distance, they could hear a faint call.

"Uncle Phil!" they called again as they followed the sound.

The sound was coming from the closet under the stairs. Ron peered around the open door into the dark closet, and there was Phil, sitting in a large box with his feet and hands poking in the air. Ron held back a laugh as he motioned for Jenny to take a look.

"Uncle Phil, are you okay?" Jenny asked.

"I'm stuck," Phil replied.

"What are you doing in here?" she asked.

"I was on my way back from the bathroom, but I guess I got lost."

"I guess you did," she said. "Ron, help him out of that box."

Ron took Phil by the hand, but when he pulled, the box came with Phil. It seemed that Phil's backside was wedged in the box. Ron pulled harder and the box tipped forward, but Phil remained stuck. Jenny took hold of the box and held it while Ron pulled again, this time freeing her uncle.

They helped Phil to his bedroom and waited while he changed from his pajamas. Then they helped him up the stairs to the family room and the waiting children.

Ron was still chuckling under his breath. "It doesn't matter what else I get for Christmas, I'm happy with my 'Phil-in-the-box,' he whispered to his wife.

"Stop it!" Jenny replied, "or that's all you will get."

❧

Leslie could hear her mother laughing as she opened the front door. She walked into Wanda's bathroom and found her standing at the sink and shaking her head.

"What's so funny?" Leslie asked.

"I . . . I . . ." Wanda tried to speak, but she couldn't get the words out.

Leslie began to chuckle. "Mom?" she asked again. "What's so funny?"

"I . . . Do you . . . It was . . ." Wanda tried to say.

Before she knew it, Leslie found herself laughing too, and she didn't even know why. After biting her tongue and taking a deep breath, she asked again. "Mom, what are you laughing at?"

Wanda was beginning to gain control, though the occasional chuckle still made its way to the surface. "Do you know what I just did?"

Leslie just shook her head for fear of laughing again if she opened her mouth.

"I was getting my pills . . ." was all Wanda could get out before she erupted into laughter once again.

Leslie couldn't hold back any longer, and she too began laughing again. The two women wrapped their arms around each other and laughed until their sides ached. Wanda even got tears in her eyes.

Finally, Leslie was able to compose herself and Wanda soon followed.

"Okay," Leslie said. "You were getting your pills . . ."

Wanda drew in a deep breath and nodded. "And I thought I had them in my hand, but just as I threw them into my mouth, I saw that they were hearing aid batteries."

Leslie smiled. "Did you spit them out?"

Wanda shook her head. "By the time it registered, it was too late," she said with a grin.

"Well, Mom, at least you've had your iron for the day," Leslie said, as she began to chuckle.

Wanda nodded. "Yeah, but I'll sure get a charge out of going to the bathroom," she said as she started to laugh again.

Funny Happens

It's hard to beat a good story, and caregiving seems to provide plenty to tell. As you work closely with your loved one, both of you will undoubtedly see and hear things that are so funny they just have to be shared. This kind of sharing can be a good thing as long as no one will be embarrassed or offended. If the story includes belittling or making fun of anyone, it is inappropriate. One way that may help determine the appropriateness of a story is to consider how you would feel if the same story was told about you in your presence. While this doesn't guarantee that no one will be offended, it's a pretty good filter.

Funny isn't funny to everyone. Individual personalities determine how people feel when a story is told about them, so be sensitive to this fact.

If you don't know how someone will react, you probably shouldn't tell the story. If your story really is that funny, you should be able to tell it without the offending parts and still give everyone a good laugh.

Laughter Is Good Medicine

Most of us have heard about research suggesting that laughter is good for the mind and body. It is reported to strengthen the immune system, boost energy, reduce pain, help chase away depression, and pro-tect against the damaging effects of stress. I've often thought about the thousands of dollars that are spent each year on medications and wondered if a good dose of appropriate humor could possibly do the same job for free. When considering the value of laughter, it makes sense to incorporate humor into all aspects of caregiving. Share humorous stories with your loved one, make light of the silly things you do, read the newspaper comics as part of your daily routine, or watch a comedy on television together. Whatever you do, find appropriate times to include humor in each day. If nothing else, you, your loved one and everyone around you will benefit from the stress-reducing effects of a good laugh.

One way that may help determine the appropriateness of a story is to consider how you would feel if the same story was told about you in your presence.

Chapter 12

"IT'S JUST A LITTLE OVERCAST"

FOCUSING ON THE GOOD TIMES

Though he was in his eighties, Tom still loved to fly. He earned his pilot's wings during the war and had been flying ever since, so when his vision began to fail, it was quite a blow. He knew he was well past the age when most men retired, but flying was his life. Now he had to give up his position as a contracted private pilot, and his role as part-time flight instructor had to be limited to teaching ground school. It wasn't long before his vision failed to the point that even teaching was too much.

Besides giving up his work, Tom found himself depending on others in ways he had never had to before. He was still able to meet his own personal needs, but he relied on others to help with meal preparation and household chores. As time passed, he began to feel like he was taking so much but giving so little. Tom was beginning to get discouraged and wondered if there was any point to his life anymore. He mentioned his feelings to one of his sons, who reminded Tom of what he had always taught his family: "Make the best of every situation and don't dwell on the negative." Tom was grateful for his son's encouragement and soon came up with a plan that would allow him to help focus on all the good things that had been and were a part of his life.

With his son as chauffeur, Tom started visiting the elementary schools where his grandchildren attended. He shared stories with the children about his days as a pilot. His presentations were very well received, and Tom was soon requested at schools throughout town. Parents soon got word of Tom's exciting stories and began inviting him to their service club meetings. In time,

Tom was speaking to several groups a week in a variety of settings. People liked his presentations so much because he had a way of relating his experiences as a pilot to life's lessons. Everyone was always amazed by his positive attitude in spite of his challenges. Tom discovered that whether speaking to a high school history class or a gathering of patients at the veteran's hospital, he was happy once again—nearly as happy as when he was flying.

Never as part of any presentation did Tom speak about the misfortune of losing his vision, his career, and much of his independence. Instead, he focused on the good times. Flying had been such an important part of his life that he used it to help create memories with his wife and children. But Tom knew, and shared with others, that the good times hadn't come because he was a pilot, but rather because he was happy. He taught that everyone has the ability to choose how they look at what life hands them. Tom was happy because he chose to be happy, and he was no different than any other happy person. Likewise, grumpy people are grumpy because they choose to be grumpy, and they are no different from other grumpy people.

Tom lived and shared into his nineties. His final presentation was made the afternoon before he quietly and happily slipped away in his sleep.

Good Leads to Good

When possible, encourage and help your loved one remain actively involved in something productive. By keeping busy, your loved one will focus on things other than his or her own ailments or frustrations. Involvement can be anything from dictating letters to a family member who lives away from home to volunteering for a local church or charity.

In some cases, remaining productive may be nothing more than the continuation of current activities, while in others, these same activities may need to be adapted or modified. Keep in mind that the time may come when some activities will need to be discontinued. As you help your loved one stay productively involved, make sure you are keeping their needs as the primary focus. Too often, well-meaning caregivers continue to include their loved one in activities or events that were once meaningful but have become difficult for them. Your insistence that participation continue could lead to embarrassment on the part of your loved one and place undue burdens on others.

Depending on your loved one's circumstances, you may need to be somewhat creative in helping him or her feel useful. If your loved one is unable to leave home, perhaps you could have a friend or family member allow you to watch his or her young child at your loved one's home for an hour or so. Projects that can be done anywhere could be done in the presence of your loved one. Older grandchildren could do their homework with a grandparent who has knowledge or interest in the subject they're studying.

For loved ones who are able to get out, there are often schools and day care centers that appreciate visits from grandparents. An occasional trip to the grocery store or to the post office may provide enough of a distraction to keep your loved one from dwelling on negative circumstances. Always keep your conversation on a positive plane, and don't provide opportunities for your loved one to turn something you said into a pity party.

Remember the Entire Journey

As with any journey, life has a beginning and an eventual end. But between the start and finish, there are a whole lot of memories. It is easy when things start getting a bit rough, to wonder why life has to include things like discouragement, tragedy, and failing health. No one, no matter their life circumstances, is able to avoid these things. Focusing on the negative in life makes for some long days for both you and your loved one.

When it comes to the challenges in your loved one's life, one of your greatest responsibilities as a caregiver is to look for the good when he or she is feeling a little down. As you regularly do this, your loved one is likely to do the same and may be less likely to dwell on the unpleasant aspects of life in the future. Sometimes, your loved one may have a hard time recalling any good, so you might want to consider it your job to remind them, sometimes even if they don't seem to want to be reminded.

If possible, have your loved one relate personal experiences from his or her life anytime he or she seems discouraged or is focused on negative thoughts. Perhaps you can ask about his or her first memory, a childhood friends, or a favorite place. By asking your loved one to share positive things, he or she will begin to think about what you're asking and will have less time to dwell on unpleasant memories. Some people don't like to talk about themselves, and if this is the case with your loved one, gather information about his or her life from family, friends, or written histories, and then ask specific questions about what you've learned. Reflect on fond memories you have, and share them with your loved one. You may find that a special experience you share with your loved one has been forgotten, but once reminded, he or she too may find a ray of sunshine in an otherwise gloomy day. Frequent discussions about good memories often spark other positive thoughts for both you and your loved one, making it easier to continue the process.

A loved one with dementia may present a few different challenges. You may have to deal with repetitiveness, where your loved one repeats the same experience over and over. But patience on your part will provide the same benefits for your loved one as he or she would receive if sharing multiple memories. Dementia can lead to confusion when trying to relate a story, and this can become frustrating for your loved one. If this happens, patiently help him or her along by filling in the blanks or simply agreeing with what is said. Even if your loved one is unable to complete an entire story, you may need to act as though you understand and appreciate what he or she shared. Until dementia reaches the later stages, long-term memory is often retained, thus allowing for meaningful discussions about events in the distant past. In the later stages of dementia, you may find that your loved one shares things that you're pretty sure aren't correct or that may have been an experience someone else had. This is not something to be alarmed about. It is normal for everyone, of every age, to remember the details of an event with less, or even different elements as the years pass. This is particularly true for those with dementia. Again, patience is the key, and in most cases, there is no harm in your agreeing with your loved one or accepting his or her version of the story.

Occasionally, you may ask a question that triggers a bad memory for your loved one. These memories may manifest themselves in your loved one as sadness or even anger. If this happens, try to redirect the conversation to a safe topic and then avoid that or similar questions in the future.

Part 5

"Death is not extinguishing the light; it is only putting
out the lamp because the dawn has come."[1]
—Rabindranath Tagore

THE FINAL
DESTINATION

There often seems to be a bit of uncertainty as the end of a long-anticipated journey approaches. As that time nears, you can look back at all that has transpired, the good with the not so good, and find your favorite parts. Still, you realize it will soon be over and wonder if things will be as you expected when you reach the end; even more, you wonder how you'll face the fact that it's actually over.

As a caregiver, the end represents many things. Not only will you face the end of your loved one's life but also the conclusion of another chapter in your own life. There are difficult emotions, decisions, and duties that are all a part of the end. The chapters in this section will help prepare you for what to expect at the end of your loved one's life.

Chapter thirteen offers suggestions that will help you face this difficult time and beyond. Chapter fourteen examines the difficult realities that are part of the end of life and how to handle them appropriately. Chapter fifteen will help you let go and say good bye.

NOTES

1. Rabindranath Tagore, quoted in Gerald O'Collins *Easter Faith: Believing in the Risen Jesus* (London: Darton, Longman & Todd, 2003), 12.

Chapter 13

"WE ARRIVED SOONER THAN I EXPECTED"

GETTING THROUGH THIS DIFFICULT TIME

*C*lara wiped a tear from her eye as she and her family drove away from the cemetery. She and Mel had been married for fifty-six years. Their life together had been good, but the past eight years had been difficult because of Mel's Alzheimer's disease. It started gradually with just a few memory problems, which weren't too difficult to deal with. But when it progressed to paranoia, things got a little harder. After a few years, Mel started requiring assistance with day-to-day things, and his dependence progressed over time. For the past nine months, he had been totally dependent on Clara to meet his needs. Their children helped out when they could, but they all lived out of town, so their availability was limited.

Each day was a struggle for both of them. Mel was unable to speak, and it had become difficult for Clara to know what he wanted. She often found herself frustrated at the end of the day.

The last month had been particularly difficult. Mel had become bedbound, so the family had arranged for a caregiver to assist Clara in meeting his needs. While this was a great help, Clara felt she was still being drained emotionally. Even small things had become a struggle. She found herself occasionally becoming impatient with Mel. This made her feel guilty, but even worse were the days when she wished Mel could just go. Clara knew in her heart she still loved her husband, but she didn't know how long she could go *on with the strain. She began to worry that these feelings would prevent her from missing Mel when he actually was gone.*

When the day arrived that Mel slipped quietly from this life, Clara sensed that something was missing. While there was a sense of relief from the stress, there was a definite void in her life. Memories of recent difficulties were soon replaced with memories of fifty-six joyous years together.

Memories

It's an interesting phenomenon, but it seems that when a personal commitment is involved in any situation, good memories seem to overshadow most unpleasant experiences. Overwhelmed caregivers often find themselves feeling guilty about their feelings toward their loved one and worry that these feelings will continue long after their loved one has passed away. But it seems to me that these feelings are actually reactions to the situation rather than deep-seated opinions about your loved one. Genuine concern and personal commitment can merge into a form of love that may not have been there before, yet it comes from the heart and is not easily overpowered. It is this love that generates lasting memories.

During periods of increased emotional stress, most people react negatively to anything that increases the stress level. Awareness of this is the greatest factor in preventing prolonged stress from creating long-term emotional challenges and bad memories for caregivers. If you realize that you are having negative feelings about your loved one, don't dwell on these feelings. Try to focus on other things, or find a way to get away from the stressful situation. The more you dwell on these unwanted feelings, the more likely you are to feel guilty about them, which can then feed a vicious cycle that may result in unpleasant memories. Caregiving includes frustration, so negative feelings are difficult to avoid, but you are the only one who can control whether or not you dwell on them.

Preparation

I've heard it said that no matter how prepared you are, you're never prepared to lose a loved one. Though circumstances leading to death vary, the end result is the same. People may have different beliefs about what happens to their loved one after death, but in spite of anyone's beliefs, death creates a separation. When a loved one dies, under any circumstances, those left behind are subject to feelings of loss and grief.

So how do you prepare for the death of your loved one? This is a difficult question to answer because circumstances differ as much as individual needs. But one important key for everyone is to know what you believe about death. Many people have a basic notion about death, but because of the unpleasant nature of the subject, they fail to truly explore and come to a real understanding of how they feel about it. Regardless of what your belief is, if you don't understand it and know what role it plays in all aspects of your life, you will have a more difficult time dealing with your grief.

Some people seem to think that avoiding the subject of death will somehow keep it from coming. One simple way to prepare for the death of a loved one is to be willing to admit that it is coming and be willing to speak about it. This includes actually saying words such as *death*, *dying*, and *dead*. Allowing yourself to speak openly about death can help you and those around you become more comfortable with the inevitable. There may even be times when it is appropriate to have similar discussions with your loved one. If he or she brings up the topic of death or makes comments suggesting he or she is ready to address the subject, you may find it a very pleasant experience that provides your loved one with an opportunity for additional preparation.

Chapter 14

"I'M NOT SURE WHAT I WAS EXPECTING"

FACING DIFFICULT REALITIES

B*en had lived a long and healthy life. Even after retirement, he continued to fill his days with worthwhile projects that often seemed to include physical labor. Ben always seemed to have the energy of a much younger man.*

Sometime around the age of eighty-five, Ilene noticed that Ben was finally beginning to slow down. She was actually grateful, because for once in their nearly sixty-five years of marriage, she could keep up with him. With less involvement in outside projects, Ben and Ilene were able to spend more time together.

Though he suffered from no major conditions, Ben's health took a noticeable turn as he approached his ninetieth birthday. His energy was gone, and his memory seemed to be slipping more than usual. At Ilene's request, their doctor ran a variety of tests on Ben, but he could find nothing of concern.

"Then what's wrong with him?" Ilene demanded upon hearing the test results.

The doctor smiled. "Wrong? Nothing is wrong. In fact, everything with him is right. Ben's worked hard all of his life, and now he's winding down. That's sometimes how it works."

Though not happy with the answer, Ilene knew the doctor was right. She had hoped a pill or some kind of therapy could help Ben regain his energy, but she knew that wasn't possible.

Over the next several months, Ben grew weaker and needed increasing assistance with his ADLs. His and Ilene's children were always there to help. Through it all, Ben remained cheerful, and Ilene remained grateful for the time she had left with him.

The day Ben couldn't get out of bed was a hard one for Ilene. She knew that meant there would be more demands on their children. But the day Ben stopped eating was even more difficult. Ilene and her children didn't want Ben to suffer, so they tried forcing him to eat. Sometimes they were successful, and sometimes, in spite of all their efforts, they couldn't get him to eat anything.

After two days of no food, Ilene became concerned and called a nurse who was a close family friend. She invited him over to speak with her and take a look at Ben.

"How can I make him eat?" was Ilene's first question to Ted.

"Why would you want to make him eat?" Ted asked.

"I know he said he didn't want to be kept alive when it was time for him to go, but he has to eat," Ilene said.

Ted thought for a minute before responding. "Ilene, does Ben need to eat, or do you need him to eat?"

"What do you mean?" Ilene asked.

"Well, how is this going to end for Ben?" Ted asked.

"You mean . . ."

Ted nodded.

"He's going to die," Ilene said hesitantly.

"We eat to stay alive," Ted said. "Are you trying to get Ben to eat so he won't die?"

"No, I just don't want him to suffer," Ilene said.

"Is there something that makes you think he's suffering right now?" Ted asked.

Ilene thought for a minute. "I guess I just don't want him starving to death."

Ted put his hand on Ilene's shoulder. "He's not starving to death, I promise," he assured. "Ben's winding down, and that means his body systems will slow down and eventually stop."

"Then he doesn't need to eat?" Ilene asked

Ted shook his head. "The only reason to feed him is if he wants to eat. It's okay to offer him food, but don't force him."

"But I still think starvation would be a terrible thing."

"It is," Ted confirmed. "But Ben isn't starving."

Ilene looked unsure.

"We eat to survive." Ted said. "Our body tells us when we need to eat for survival by making us hungry."

"Ben isn't hungry, is he?" Ilene asked.

Ted shook his head. "No, he isn't. Your desire to feed him is to relieve your suffering. I know it's difficult to watch because we naturally assume that Ben must be hungry."

"I guess if he was hungry, he'd eat when we offered him food," Ilene admitted.

"You can continue to offer, but don't force him, and don't get upset if he refuses," Ted said.

Ilene told her children about her conversation with Ted. Together, they agreed that Ted's explanation made sense. They continued to offer Ben food, and he continued to refuse it. Occasionally, they had to remind themselves that he would eat if he wanted to. Ben seemed to enjoy a drink of cold water several times a day, but he had no interest in food.

After two weeks with no food, Ben began to refuse the water he had seemed to appreciate. Ted confirmed by telephone that Ben's time was near. The next day, Ben took his last breath with Ilene holding his hand in hers. She was grateful that his final days were pleasant ones for him and for everyone involved in his care.

Natural Defenses

Most caregivers have a difficult time with the idea that as their loved one nears the end of life, they will often stop eating and drinking. They have images of severe hunger pangs and needless suffering by their loved one, all because they refuse to eat. The fact is, as the body prepares for death, it systematically slows down and eventually terminates all functions. The length of time this process takes depends on the cause of death, but it can last anywhere from one day to two weeks or more. This is a natural process, and the body has natural defense mechanisms designed to allow the process to occur without suffering. Most of us have experienced going an extended time without food yet not feeling hungry. This often happens when we're preoccupied, busy working on a project, or are perhaps not feeling well. This is similar to what your loved one experiences when his or her appetite decreases. Of course, *we* eventually need to eat to maintain our energy level, but an aging loved one has decreasing activity levels and therefore a decreased need for fuel. The loss of appetite in a dying loved one is part of the natural process and though sometimes difficult for you to think about, is not generally a harsh or difficult experience for him or her.

It Happens

No matter how hard you might try, you can't stop the natural course of human life. Those who are fortunate enough to make it to old age will still reach the end one day. Certainly things can be done to delay it for a while, but ultimately, death happens. Most of us fight it because there is so much that is unknown. Even those whose belief system prepares them for death still face a number of unknowns because they, like everyone else, have never experienced death before. It is not unusual for you, your loved one, or others to be resistant to the idea of death. For some, this resistance is as natural as death itself. Do not be too hard on yourself or others for wanting to prolong the inevitable for as long as possible. Ultimately, simple efforts to extend life at this point will likely have little if any impact on your loved one, but the attempts may be helpful and sometimes necessary for those who feel the need to do all they can. Measures taken to prolong life in these situations are not usually inappropriate unless they go against the wishes of your loved one or those authorized to make end-of-life decisions for them or are considered by competent medical opinion to cause unnecessary suffering.

Honoring Wishes

Many people determine in advance the measures to be taken at the end of their life. Living wills or other forms of advance directives are legal documents that direct medical care in situations where death is likely. These types of documents are becoming more common and generally make things easier for caregivers when a loved one nears death. Occasionally, caregivers face situations where their personal feelings conflict with the desires of their loved one. If you find yourself in this situation, you have the moral and legal obligation to comply with the expressed wishes of your loved one. Your opinion should never override his or her desires. Honoring the wishes of your loved one should always be your aim.

If you are the caregiver of someone who has not made any legal declaration regarding end-of-life medical treatment, you should encourage him or her to do so. Your loved one's physician can assist you in finding and or filling out the correct forms for your state. Home health or hospice agencies as well as long-term care facilities will also be able to assist you.

Occasionally, caregivers find themselves in a situation where their loved one has not taken the steps to make a legal declaration, nor to authorize anyone to make end-of-life decisions on his or her behalf. In most states, when there is no advance directive and no designated medical power of attorney, the next-of-kin as defined by that state would be the person with the authority to make those decisions. If you find yourself in this situation, you should do your best the make the decisions you feel your loved one would have made on his or her own. If you are aware of someone who may understand your loved one better than you in regards to your loved one's feelings about the end of life, then it may be wise to seek this person's advice. Bear in mind that seeking advice from too many people can lead to more confusion on your part. It is always appropriate to consider the advice of others, but in the end, it is up to you. As long as you are sincerely making every effort to act on your loved one's behalf as you feel he or she would have acted, then your decisions will be the correct ones. This will leave no room for guilt, now or in the future.

Chapter 15

"WE'RE HERE!"

LETTING GO AND SAYING GOOD-BYE

When Judith was released from the hospital, she had regained much of her ability to provide self-care, though she still required supervision for some tasks. She responded better than most after her type of traumatic brain injury, though she was left unable to speak. But Judith found it easy to communicate using her wide smile and piercing eyes. Everyone loved her.

Over the years, Judith's health gradually declined, and her assistance needs increased. Her two children were grateful for the help they were able to obtain to assist in meeting their mother's needs. They seemed to have no difficulty finding competent and compassionate caregivers. Eventually, Judith was admitted to a care facility. The staff there fell in love with her immediately. Judith always had a gleam in her eye that made everyone around her feel happy. But after a few months, the smile was seldom seen and the sparkle in her eye was dimmed.

It was a difficult day when Tom (the facility director) called Judith's son, John, and arranged for a time to discuss Judith's declining state of health. John said he would contact his sister, Rebecca, and invite her to the meeting scheduled for the following day.

At the meeting, Tom explained that it was time to make some difficult decisions concerning Judith's future because she had not previously made her wishes known regarding end-of-life care. He told them that their mother's appetite had decreased, that she had begun refusing her medications, and seemed to be having difficulty swallowing—all signs that death was *approaching. John expressed his desire to simply keep their mother comfortable, but Rebecca felt they should intervene in any way they could. What had started as a calm discussion soon turned into a heated argument between the siblings. Tom suggested that everyone go home and give serious thought to the situation and meet again in a few days. In the meantime, he said he would contact Judith's physician for her opinion. Tom hoped that John and Rebecca would resolve their differences before the next meeting.*

The subsequent meeting ended with no resolution. Judith's doctor confirmed that she was within six months of death but would say no more than that. Rebecca felt that they should make every effort to extend beyond that six-month window. John could see no point in prolonging what he felt was a life void of quality. When they asked Tom what he would do if it were his mother, he wisely replied, "She's not my mother. She's yours."

John and Rebecca continued in disagreement for several weeks. During that time, Judith was diagnosed with a bladder infection and was treated with antibiotics. A subsequent infection a few days later prompted Rebecca to suggest that poor nutrition could be the cause. She raised the question of tube feedings for her mother. John was completely opposed.

One night, when she and John were visiting Judith, Rebecca stayed behind after John went home. She spent the night at her mother's bedside, holding her hand and talking to her. Though Judith's eyes no longer communicated as well as they used to, it was clear to Rebecca what they were saying.

John was surprised to see Rebecca when he stopped in to see Judith on his way to work the next morning. He didn't say anything because he didn't want to get into an argument.

"It's okay," Rebecca said after a prolonged awkward silence.

"What's okay?" John asked.

"I'm ready to let go," she said.

John was shocked. "Are you sure?" he asked.

"I'm sure," Rebecca confirmed. "It's time to tell Mom good-bye."

John embraced his sister. They felt that they needed to stay with their mother a bit longer. By midafternoon, Judith's breathing had become irregular.

Just after dusk, Judith passed away. Both John and Rebecca had been able to tell their mother good-bye.

Individual Departure

Though we know everyone will die, we don't usually know when or how death will come. Still, as a caregiver, you probably have some idea about how your loved one's life will end. This is due in part to your aware-ness of his or her health status and its rate of decline. But even with that knowledge, the exact time is still unknown to you, which forces you to watch for the signs that death is approaching. As you watch for the warn-ing signs, be aware that they are general in nature and that death is a very individual thing.

I have observed that often, the elderly leave this life the way they lived it. If they were private people—the kind that kept aches and pains and illnesses to themselves—they will often die in private when no one is around. Those who were open about how they felt and shared freely will often die while family and friends are gathered at the bedside. I have seen families gathered around a loved one for days on end to be sure their loved one didn't die alone, only to have him or her die during the brief moment the family slipped out for a bite to eat. I have also witnessed the opposite, where a loved one hangs on for days and passes away once everyone in the family has gathered. While these observations by no means constitute any kind of rule, they should help you realize that your loved one will go when it's most comfortable for them. Be sensitive to them and try to provide an atmosphere that meets their needs. This can be easily accom-plished by allowing your loved one time to be alone occasionally, rather than having a constant vigil at their side. Once you determine what your loved one prefers, you can act accordingly. You may find that your loved one likes a balance of both.

Their Time

Most caregivers end up in that role because of their concern for the one needing care. This concern generally deepens over time, and if it was not originally based on love, it can evolve to that point. This makes it dif-ficult to let your loved one go when death approaches. This is a natural response, not only for caregivers but also for anyone who is close to your loved one. But remember that this is your loved one's time. As hard as it may be to let him or her go, it's the right thing to do when the end is clearly there. Occasionally, you'll hear someone say something to a loved one like, "You can't go—I just can't live without you." While such a sen-timent may be understandable, it is usually spoken with no thought of reality. There is some evidence that these types of statements and even unspoken feelings can prolong the life of a dying person, but they do so for only a short time. Ultimately, the loved one will die, and everyone will be left to carry on without them. A person in the process of dying should be allowed to go through that process without others making them feel guilty for doing so. You owe it to your loved one to let them go when it's time.

I've always been taught that hearing is the last sense to go when a person dies, and my experience leads me to believe that is true. With that in mind, be aware of what is being said in your loved one's presence. Keep conversation positive at the bedside or in the room with them. Encourage the sharing of good memories or uplifting stories. Be sure your loved one is included in any conversation in their presence, even if they are unable to respond.

Your Time

While the dying process may belong to your loved one, there is a place for you. Your role, or rather your opportunity, is to experience the reverence and intimacy that surrounds death. Too many people dwell so much on their loss that they fail to recognize or remember what they've received. Many years ago as a young nurse, I found myself attracted to the bedside of patients who were dying. At first, I thought that there must be something wrong with me, but then I discovered that the attraction came from a familiar feeling. Though at first I couldn't identify the feeling, I recognized it as comfortable and desirable. It wasn't until months later while attending the birth of a child that I realized I was experiencing the same feeling then. I believe I was feeling life at its ebb and flow. You do not need to adhere to any particular belief to recognize the feelings present when death is near, but you do need to decide how to deal with them when they come. There is an opportunity to experience something wonderful if you will allow it to happen.

Another part of your time includes grieving for the loss of your loved one. Grief is natural, necessary, and personal. It can be either positive or negative. As you grieve, be aware of what you are feeling and what that grief is doing for you. Grief becomes negative when it isolates you from others, consumes your life, or debilitates you. Negative grief prevents you from remembering your loved one because you find it too painful to think about them. Positive grief, on the other hand, is enriching and allows for enlightening reflection on the life of your loved one. Everyone grieves in his or her own way and time. Plan to make your time positive and uplifting. Of course there will be times of sorrow when the loss may seem too great, but these times should be carefully and thoughtfully spaced by periods of joy for the life that was lived and the part you played in it.

The best way to manage your grief is to keep the good memories close to your heart, share your newly gained experience with others, spend time with those closest to you, and never forget your loved one.

CONCLUSION

No matter how much information is provided for caregivers, there will always be questions. This book was not written as an all-inclusive authority on the subject of caregiving, but hopefully you have gained enough insight that you will have an idea of how to proceed in any situation.

While the basic rules of caregiving are the same for the majority of circumstances, as in all things, there will be exceptions. I have found that always worrying about the exceptions makes an anxious caregiver. Imagine trying to enjoy a family vacation when all you can think about is the possibility of a flat tire or a forgotten hotel reservation. Whether on a vacation or in the care setting, this type of anxiety makes it difficult to adjust to changing needs and makes the whole journey miserable for everyone involved. The best preparation for the unexpected is a simple recognition that it will be encountered, and when it is, you can deal with it.

As you move forward on your caregiving journey, you may speak to people who do not agree with all of the ideas offered in this book, and that's okay. In fact, they may offer suggestions that are better than mine. The real issue is the care of your loved one. No individual or organization has an exclusive on the right method of caring for a loved one. Be willing to embrace helpful information from any reliable source.

The fact that you have read this book indicates that you care about your loved one and have a desire to do what is best for him or her. My hope is that I have provided some tools that will help you fulfill that desire.

Go enjoy the journey!

ABOUT THE AUTHOR

Todd F. Cope grew up in a family of thirteen children. As the youngest, he quickly learned that service was the best way to get along with others. After graduating from high school, Todd traveled to Western Australia to work as a missionary. It was there that he met a missionary from New Zealand who would later become his wife.

Todd and Denise were married in New Zealand, where they lived for two years before returning to the United States so he could continue his education. Together they raised four children and are now experiencing the joys of being grandparents.

It was his desire to help others that led Todd to pursue a career in nursing. Working as a registered nurse for more than twenty-five years, he has had the opportunity of working in a variety of settings, but the majority of his career has involved caring for the elderly. In his spare time, Todd enjoys running, gardening, and spending time with his family.

Todd's love for writing dates back to the fourth grade, when he won a poetry writing contest. He continued to be honored for his essays, poetry, and prose throughout his school career. Todd has published many articles on a variety of subjects in several forums, including the *Ensign* and *New Era* magazines. He is the author of four published novels, most notably *The Shift*, a self-published work that inspired the CBS television movie *The Last Dance*, starring Maureen O'Hara.